Praise for **Blindsided**

"Mark Roser's well-crafted book is beyond inspiring. It brought not only flowing tears, but a delight in seeing how God answered his deepest questions. Having lost our precious Kayla in an accident, I am also able to rejoice that God chooses young radiant souls like Ethan and my daughter to reach their generation for Christ. As Jesus said, 'Truly, I tell you, unless a kernel of wheat falls to the ground and dies, it remains only a single seed. But if it dies, it produces many seeds' (John 12:24). *Blindsided* will help you seize every opportunity—even the difficult ones—to spread Christ's glorious gospel and reach 'a thousand Ethans.'"
—**Julia Kay Duerler**, author of *She Had No Regrets*

"A searing and honest look at the pain and grief Mark Roser and his family experienced. Before the accident, Mark was known as a minister who wrote and taught on God's sovereignty. One of the toughest theological questions we will ever face is the question of why there is evil and suffering. There is no sugar coating a father's grief as he asks, 'Why did God allow my son to die?' and as he says, 'Preaching it is a whole lot easier than living it!' Roser is a modern Job."
—**Dr. Gary Sweeten**, Founder, LifeWay Counseling Centers

"Roser's beautiful, poignant book made me laugh and cry and feel deeply, not only for them in their loss, but coming to terms with that most haunting of questions about suffering, *Why, God?* It also helped me process my own experience of loss, forgiveness, and making sense of tragedy in life."
—**Suzanne E. Shaw**, PsyD, MFT, Marriage and Family Therapist

"Having lost a beloved seventeen-year-old daughter in a tragic accident, we connected with Mark's amazing book that describes the place where we ourselves lived, as he put into words the questions and feelings of every parent who loses a child. We have known Mark and Pat for more than twenty-five years, as Mark was our church's inaugural mission guest speaker, and we have watched the Rosers live out their love for God when life hurts."
—**Pastor Gary and Mary Trenum**
Founders of Victory Christ

MARK C. ROSER

Blindsided

A Journey from Tragic Loss to Triumphant Love

PARACLETE PRESS
BREWSTER, MASSACHUSETTS

2021 First Printing

Blindsided: A Journey from Tragic Loss to Triumphant Love

Copyright © 2021 by Uttermost Missions

ISBN 978-1-64060-652-4

The Paraclete Press name and logo (dove on cross) are trademarks of Paraclete Press.

Library of Congress Cataloging-in-Publication Data
Names: Roser, Mark C., 1958- author.
Title: Blindsided : a journey from tragic loss to triumphant love /
  Mark C. Roser.
Description: Brewster, Massachusetts : Paraclete Press, 2021. | Summary:
  "After the death of his son, the author kept his sanity by writing, as
  he wrestled with questions as profound as life itself"-- Provided by
  publisher.
Identifiers: LCCN 2020042085 (print) | LCCN 2020042086 (ebook) | ISBN
  9781640606524 | ISBN 9781640606531 (epub) | ISBN 9781640606548 (pdf)
Subjects: LCSH: Children--Death--Religious aspects--Christianity. |
  Grief--Religious aspects--Christianity. | Bereavement--Religious
  aspects--Christianity. | Roser, Mark C., 1958- | Roser, Ethan,
  1997-2017.
Classification: LCC BV4907 .R65 2021 (print) | LCC BV4907 (ebook) | DDC
  248.8/66092--dc23
LC record available at https://lccn.loc.gov/2020042085
LC ebook record available at https://lccn.loc.gov/2020042086

10 9 8 7 6 5 4 3 2 1

Published by Paraclete Press
Brewster, Massachusetts
www.paracletepress.com

Printed in the United States of America

CONTENTS

PROLOGUE

A Dark Weight

....

"I have a place in God's plan."

....

A COLD GUST OF AIR blows into my office, sending a paper gliding to the floor. Reaching over my desk, I shut the window with a thud and place a paperweight on the stack of papers that document my catastrophe. I lift the paperweight a second time—it's about four pounds—far less than the sixteen-pound weight that broke my heart.

I still can't believe it happened!

Slumping back into my leather chair, I roll forward to my desk and wake my PC. The screen reads: "April 29, 2:32 a.m." I resist the urge to go online and read more articles about it. The newspapers offer no answer to my question.

The house is so quiet I hear myself sigh. Then, as if from an adjacent bedroom, the sound of Ethan's voice plays in my head.

"Bottle," I hear him call as if were yesterday, rather than years ago. Pat nicknamed him Baa Lamb, because his infant voice sounded like a wee lamb's, and when he woke at 5:30 a.m. he loved to sip warm milk out of his bottle. A year and a half old, he kept calling out; his initially pleasant requests increased in volume and pitch every couple of minutes he waited. "Bottle . . . Bottle . . . BOTTLE!" When at last the warm milk arrived, he always said, "Tanku."

"Daddy," I imagine him say. Oh, I'd like to think "Daddy" was his first word, but growing up in Zimbabwe with an African nanny—was Ethan's first word even in English?

"Baba." Yes, that's it. He called me Baba, meaning "father" in the Shona language. Often, I heard his voice saying, ever so sweetly, "Baba, I love you!"

Ethan was ten years old when we returned to America, and he loved soccer, Africa's favorite sport. His first soccer team in America was Orange Crush. As the ball went up and down the field, he was always in the middle of the cloud of dusty boys. Teasing him, I said with a rough accent, "Your African name is, 'Eka Boom Ba,' meaning he who strikes the round thing.'" He laughed, and I encouraged him to play for God's glory. Before one game, I suggested, "Let's pray you get a goal today."

"I can get goals without praying," Ethan replied.

"Well, I know you can, but could there be reasons why we'd ask?"

"So we don't get cocky!" he said, giggling.

That day he had two goals, the first one on a lucky bounce. After that, he always wanted me to pray. Ethan's dream was to play professional soccer, and he pursued it with a passion. As a sophomore, he played varsity at Mason High School and helped his team go undefeated. They were ranked number one in America. His club team, Cincinnati United Premier (CUP), was also a top team in America. Playing in weekend tournaments became a staple of life for him, and it kept me busy as the years ticked away like the final minutes of a competitive game.

But tonight, the minutes seem eternal as if time has stopped and the game is over.

That first summer after we came back from Africa, a church up the road had a Vacation Bible School. More than a hundred kids attended, and Ethan loved going. The week ended with an ice cream evening with the parents. Everybody knew Ethan, the boy from Africa, who won the award for quoting more Bible verses than any kid. Then, in his junior year of high school, a greater love than soccer completely captured his heart. At church Ethan reported on Frontier Ranch:

> As cliché as it is, my week at Frontier Ranch was one of the best weeks of my life. Most people feel this way because Frontier is usually the place where they start their relationship with Jesus. But the reasons I'll remember that week are very different. At camp I had time to be still and to bask in the authority of God and focus on His almighty plan. I have a place in God's plan. At camp, I realized I have one last chance to impact my 4,000 friends at Mason High School. But I'm not a preacher. I'm just Ethan. I'm that kid in your math class. But I want to bring the presence of Jesus to my classmates because they need the Lord.

Well, son, you certainly found a way to do that, and as I glance at your picture on my desk, I realize I should've known years ago your life would not be normal. I should have recorded more of what you said.

The silent house and his lingering voice in the house summon me, *Write while it's all still fresh in your mind.*

I open a blank document, flexing my shoulders on the back of my office chair, then stretching my arms above my head, I ask, "Where does one begin?"

"Dad, you need a good hook!" Last summer Ethan had read a draft of *My African Dream* and said, "Start with your long drive from South Africa through Matabeleland at night, where the dissidents were roaming the bush with AK-47 rifles!" Many times, Ethan's insights and words left me spellbound. Often, I joked with him, "One day I will write a book on the sayings of Ethan." He gave me his "Oh, really!" look.

The dreadful irony of it—Pat and I happily wrote our memoirs, titled *My African Dream,* and now in sorrow I could write *My American Nightmare.*

Looking at that ugly round paperweight next to his picture on my desk, I imagine it flying in the air. Swiftly, it strikes the stack of papers, tearing into them like a hungry cacodemon. It scatters fragments, floating in the air all around me, and my feelings, sharp as rotating sawblades, swirl about me, cutting away at my flesh, ever more deeply.

Oh, God, I wish to die!

Taking a deep breath, I shut down my PC. But I can't stop the sense that I'm left to slowly bleed out. And a rage rises within me against the darkness, for though I'm surrounded on three sides by shelves full of thick books on theology, I can't stop asking God one question: "WHY?"

· 1 ·

A Knock at the Door

(A WEEK AGO)

ETHAN'S TWEET: *"The lady at Chipotle sneaks me three scoops of chicken. I'm about to hibernate. Life is good."*

ENTERING THE KITCHEN from the garage, I catch a whiff of last night's burnt popcorn. Pat sits at the island with a bowl of salad and forks a piece of lettuce. I swing the microwave door shut.

"We'll have Ethan's room carpeted by the time he's home for the summer."

"Are you hungry?" she asks, looking over at me.

"Just thirsty," I reply, and I grab a bottle of tea from the fridge. "Fred's guys did a nice job laying the floor. Far better than I could've done. You know, I think it looks like real wood."

"Sort of—I'm not crazy about it," and her fork goes hunting again. "I would've liked to see it in a browner shade."

It took two trips to Floor and Décor in my Ford Ranger to transport that flooring. I took it all back when I couldn't install it properly. Then, I had to buy and transport it all a second time.

"Well, it's a little late for that now," and I pop open my drink.

"When does Ethan get home?" Pat asks.

"He'll be here in three weeks."

"I miss him being in the house."

"Yeah, you pour yourself into your kids, and they leave you for college and get married."

We have had a wedding two years running. Our oldest, Johnathan, married first, and then Nathan got married six months ago. Elesha has her own house, and Ethan is now at college.

"Well, that's how it's meant to be," Pat says, as she takes her bowl to the sink.

Well, I still have Pat. My brown-eyed, brunette beauty always gives me another perspective. Adventuresome and intelligent, ever active, she has aged like fine wine. Having turned sixty last month, she maintains an attractive figure. I imagine that's because of all the salads she eats.

"You want to watch a movie together?" I ask.

"Let's watch one in about thirty minutes," she says, and she loads the dishwasher.

When the kids were home, weekends meant candy and a movie. Lord knows, I need a quiet Saturday after another full week of finishing our lower level, and down the steps I go to our basement and maneuver around a pile of baseboards. Before Ethan left for college, my boy and I did the stud walls for his new bedroom and his own bathroom. We got good at hammering nails into the two-by-fours, but in the process the hammers sometimes found our thumbs. I said, "I know why construction workers cuss more than accountants." We laughed.

Sipping cold tea, I savor the thought that Ethan will soon be home for the summer, and I wonder, is he eating right now, studying, or training? I'm sure he's using his time well. His high school coach,

Paul Reedy, wrote in his recommendation for Ethan, that in twenty-five years of coaching, he never had a player with a stronger work ethic than Ethan. With school and club soccer, Ethan still maintained a 3.6 GPA.

We are new empty nesters, and I don't like it. We did, however, effectively transition our four children from Zimbabwe to America, this wonderful land of opportunity, and now with the youngest off to college, it is easy for Pat and me to travel overseas. As I walk back up the steps, my knees remind me that I'm climbing the hill to age sixty this year, or maybe it's the months of doing renovations, or maybe it's Daylight Savings? We never had that in Africa. Whatever it is, I'm finished for the day even though it's only five p.m.

One last thing I'll do—a church in Texas needs more copies of my book *God's Sovereignty*: "Do bad things just happen to people? Are thorns dealt out like a deck of cards?" Questions on the book's back stare at me. Written during the long crisis in Zimbabwe, my book has helped people face hard times. The Bible teaches that God rules over every detail of our lives. There is nothing outside his control. We can trust him no matter what. For some reason, the bigger theological questions attract me. But writing on complex themes is time consuming, and my itinerating and doing mission trips keep me busy.

I finish packing the final copy in a box to mail on Monday and head for the shower.

The hot water soothes my shoulders.

Ten minutes later in bed, I'm surfing a handful of local TV stations. Pat joins me, sitting on the bedspread. We watch a story about a tight-knit Armenian family in Turkey, three generations living under one roof. Religious persecution, however, separates the father and son. Flashbacks of happier childhood days in Istanbul, rolling flat bread and playing with the girl next door. The story moves slowly as Middle Eastern music fades out again. . . .

"Someone is knocking at the door. Will you get it?" Pat asks.

I didn't even hear them knocking. I jump into my tracksuit and stride through the hall. Outside the dining room window, I see a police cruiser sitting in our driveway.

What is this about? Only once before did the police come to our house—when I was the victim of Identity Theft. I hurry to open the door. A well-built officer stands in the entrance.

"Are you Ethan Roser's father?" he asks in a serious tone.

"Yes." My heart races.

"Your son has been in an accident."

"Is he hurt?"

"I don't know," and he shakes his head. "Call this officer in Chicago," and he hands me a slip of paper.

My God, what's happening? Please don't let Ethan be hurt badly.

I picture his Cavalier smashed on a busy expressway and him in an ambulance, being raced to a local hospital. In the pit of my stomach, I feel sick. Looking at the officer, I don't know what to say.

"I'm sorry," the officer says in a soft voice, and then he turns and leaves.

Gripping the slip of paper, I run back to the bedroom. "Ethan has been in an accident!"

Pat frantically reaches for her cell phone on her nightstand.

"I missed a call," she says, struggling to breathe, "with a Chicago area code!" Her hands shaking, she presses her phone to call the number.

Everything is moving too fast. I'm exploding. I can't be still. Rushing to my office with the slip of paper the officer gave me, I dial the number on my Captel phone. A voice mail answers.

"I'm Ethan's father." Balancing myself with a hand on my desk, I press the phone to my mouth. "Is my son hurt bad? Please phone me now!"

Putting the phone back on the receiver, my body tenses. I abruptly recall a nightmare I had of Ethan leaving me. It surges to the front of my mind, and all the horror hits me of the dreaded words spoken in my nightmare: "He's leaving you for eternity."

"Oh, God," I shout, "You're not taking my son from me—are you? No, don't!"

Terror encircles me, and I pace between the living room and the hallway, screaming, "No, God, no! Please NO! PLEASE don't take my son from me!"

· 2 ·

Leaving Me?

(TEN MONTHS EARLIER)

....

"I'm never going to let you die!"

....

"WE DID THIS!" Ethan says, standing on the driveway pad with boxes around us. There's a *wow!* in his voice as he looks at the gravel beneath us.

He and I had built a thirty-five-foot-long retaining wall and with forty tons of gravel filled in the sloping mound where he stands; strenuous work, but we doubled our parking area.

Elesha comes down the driveway in her black Jeep Compass and pulls to a stop next to a couple of large packed boxes. We quickly put them in her hatchback. Ethan then climbs inside Elesha's back seat, holding his pillow like we're heading out of town for a weekend of soccer games. But today our boy is headed out of the nest, bound for Dallas Baptist University.

I hop into Ethan's car to drive it while he sleeps. Branded by dents on both sides, his 2001 silver Chevy Cavalier had been my mom's car. She put the bigger dent on the driver's side before she stopped driving, and the other door got banged at a Young Life meeting. "Let's not make them pay," Ethan had said, and we left it dented. He didn't care how it looked, and for me it was all about what was under the hood, an engine with plenty of life. As I start the engine, the odometer now reads a mere 42,211 miles. Next to me, the passenger seat holds a laundry basket filled with Ethan's shoes, placed on top of a box of books. His back seat is crammed with more boxes and a black suitcase. On top of the suitcase are piles of colorful shirts on white plastic hangers, spread out like freshly cut flowers.

Elesha pulls out of the driveway. I follow her, convoy style. The old Chevy gobbles up the miles, like my mom, age ninety-two. I envision this car lasting Ethan all four of his years in Dallas.

We arrive in D-town to a sizzling heat, 103 degrees, and in our hotel room, we crank up the air conditioning. That evening, we watch the Rangers play baseball. A thunderstorm rolls in and breaks up the heat and the game, but we add another park to our resume. Two summers ago, Ethan and I began visiting baseball parks around the country. We made trips to Wrigley Field, PNC Park, Busch Stadium, and Great American Park.

The next day, we move Ethan's stuff into his dorm room, and then it hits me—we must say goodbye. Ethan and Elesha look surprised. I must tell them why I'm crying, and I hurry into the room.

"Remember our overnight train ride from Johannesburg to Cape Town? Ethan, you were six and so excited when we arrived. You called me over and stood on a chair. 'Look,' you said, peering into my eyes. 'I'm taller than you.' Then you said, 'I'm never going to forget you. I'm never going to let you die,' and you gave me the sweetest kiss."

Elesha's eyes moisten, and she puts her arm around me. Ethan is quiet, his face thoughtful as he absorbs the moment like a tree whose roots are often saturated by good rains.

The next day, Elesha and I leave Ethan in Dallas and drive back to Cincinnati.

The summer before Ethan left for college, I explained to him that when the youngest leaves home, parents feel the loss more intensely because it marks the end of an era for them. I said, in jest, "You'll have to hang around the house longer than your siblings." He looked at me, knowingly, pleased that I had cloaked my deep feelings in a playful way lest I make him sad when he needed to be excited about all the opportunities ahead of him.

Since we are a tight-knit family and have lived away from relatives for many years, I particularly feel the loss of Ethan's presence in the house, because for the past five years, I've spent oodles of time with him. My life is bound up with his life as tightly as a knot.

Back home in Cincinnati, Pat and I Skype with Ethan, and we talk about his growing desire to transfer to Wheaton College. Then we just look at one another and smile, Pat and I, lying in our bed in Loveland and Ethan lying on the top of a bunk bed in Dallas.

"We are going to come down and watch you play," I say, and we sign off.

October in Dallas, Ethan picks us up at the airport in his Cavalier, talking and driving, happy to see Mom and Dad. It's been three months, our longest separation ever.

We go to a real Texas barbeque restaurant where his team recently ate. We sit in a wooden booth. Plates of ribs and sides of mashed potatoes and green beans arrive at our table. I've always enjoyed giving Ethan food. After soccer practice, I'd heat up his dinner, and we'd sit and talk while he ate. It was at one dinner during his junior year when he told me, "I want to be a minister."

As Ethan eats a rib, that conversation replays itself in my mind: "I thought God gifted me to play soccer, but I see he's given me other gifts. I understand the Bible, and I can articulate it and make connections between passages that genuinely excite me." "There are other vocations besides ministry that honor God," Pat pointed out. "I know," replied Ethan, "but I have a passion for it, and serving God is the only thing that I could do that would have a lasting effect."

Now here he is at DBU, studying for the ministry and playing soccer.

Ethan finishes a slab and takes a napkin with one hand and goes for his drink with the other. I reckon it's time to talk again about his desire to transfer to Wheaton.

"Maybe you should finish your freshman year here, because of your scholarship money."

"Wheaton offers a two-thousand-dollar scholarship." Ethan looks over at me. "It's for interns who do summer ministry." He then focuses on his mashed potatoes.

"That helps, but Wheaton is far more expensive."

"I wrote to the Vineyard and Crossroads about summer internships, but I haven't heard anything back yet. But four years of internships would be eight thousand dollars." There's a twinkle in his eyes.

"Well, for your summer internship, you could promote our book at churches," I suggest.

"Ethan, I can see you talking about your years in Africa. You'd be good at it!" Pat says.

People are naturally attracted to Ethan. He's 160 pounds of muscle in sculpted calves, thighs, and a six-pack abdomen. His narrow upper body rests on a five-foot-ten Italian frame. His head is topped off with brown wavy hair, cut short on the sides, atop a handsome Irish face. His skin is clear with a few faint freckles. He also features a friendly smile and unforgettable hazel brown eyes that dance in celebration of life.

"Ethan, forget college. I could train you myself. We'd travel and you'd read books on theology." I smile. "Then you wouldn't have any debt at all."

I've talked to Ethan before about taking over our homegrown mission.

As he processes my semi-serious proposition about hands-on training, his eyebrows rise, then his facial muscles crinkle, and he chuckles hard. A family two booths away smiles over at us. His laugh is the contagious type that makes you laugh too, even if you have no idea what he's laughing about. In his high school yearbook, he was voted the one with the best laugh.

"Dad, I want to play soccer! But I'll help you with the mission work after I graduate. I'm talking with the coach at Wheaton. Here's an email I plan to send him. Tell me what you think."

Ethan hands me his phone, and he goes for the soft-serve ice cream machine.

> Coach, I've really been praying and seeking guidance from God and my family on what I should do. I don't want to make the mistake of just leaving DBU based on my own judgment and emotions and it not be God's will. But I feel in my spirit that it was right for me to pursue Wheaton. None of us can truly understand the complexity of what God is doing in our lives, although sometimes I think we all wish we could take a quick glance at His cheat sheet.

"I think it's a good email," I say to Ethan as he returns with a bowl of ice cream.

Also, I think he's got me on board, and I'll be helping him transfer. At least, he'll be closer to home—four, not twelve hours away. When we drop Ethan off at his dorm, it is no wonder he wants to transfer. The parking lot is empty. The campus looks like a ghost town since most of the students are from the Dallas area and go home for the weekend. Ethan longs for community, and before our week with him is over, he tells his DBU coach that he plans on transferring to Wheaton College.

* * *

IN JANUARY 2017, I drive Ethan to Wheaton. The campus occupies several streets with lots of green space and many mature trees. We slowly drive past Wheaton's football stadium and stop at their soccer stadium. I imagine I'll watch Ethan play many games here. Several buildings have a historical feel, and the date 1860, the college's first year, catches my eye. At Fischer Hall, I proudly help him move his things into his dorm room on the second floor.

Inside the student recreational building, a special mission display features former Wheaton graduates Jim Elliot and Nate Saint, missionaries who were martyred in Ecuador for their faith.

We shoot a game of pool and decide to go for a bite to eat. It's cold in Chicago. Compared to Dallas, it's frigid. But Ethan says he'll get used to it. He's a third culture kid (TCK). That's what sociologists call kids who spent their formative years away from their parents' homeland. Third culture kids cope better with change and are unusually accepting of others who are different. Ethan has also avoided the downside of being a TCK, since he spent ten years in one place, instead of moving to a new place every couple of years.

After two days together, Ethan is waiting in his car while I board a Greyhound. My bus pulls away, and minutes later, he phones.

"Dad, I really appreciate you bringing me. It was really good of you." The following day, he texts me: "The number of theology classes is incredible! There are so many interesting ones. They even have classes where you just examine David's life."

"You will love that. I know God had you transfer to Wheaton. I'm excited for you!"

A month later, in February, I make sure to spend a night in Chicago before my connecting flight to Nepal. Ethan and I have dinner. I can see he's happier. He drops me off at my hotel, and I watch him turn his car around as we wave at one another a couple of times. Then he pulls onto the street, out of my sight. I think I'll be spending a lot of time in Chicago, flying overseas for mission trips out of O'Hare rather than JFK.

Back from my trip to Nepal, I have odd experiences waking up. Over a two-week period in March, I repeatedly have these disturbing thoughts drifting through my mind right as I awaken: *I have four children, not three. I speak their names, "Johnathan, Elesha, Nathan, and Ethan." And I assure myself that's four, not three.* The naming and counting of my children as I regain consciousness happens on a handful of occasions. Strange and unsettling. Why would anyone wonder how many children they have? I've had thoughts float through my mind before as I woke up, but never this clear and never the same thoughts repeating themselves.

Two weeks later, I wake up from a nightmare. In it, Ethan says, "I'm leaving you." "Why are you leaving me?" I ask. Before I get an answer, I plead in terror, "Please don't leave me!" Then in my dream I hear these words come from beyond Ethan: "He's leaving you for eternity." The words strike me with a terrible finality, and I struggle against awful feelings of emptiness.

Once fully awake, I raise myself up on my elbow. Whatever that was, a nightmare or a shadowy demon, it struck my heart with enormous alarm. *What's wrong with me that I'd have a dream like that?* Is that how I feel about Ethan leaving for college?

When the older kids went to college, Pat and I couldn't see them for months at a time. Maybe the trauma of past separations has caught up with me now that the last one is at college.

It's April 15, 2017, and I pray for my children by name as I do every morning. I ask God to protect them and fulfill his plans for their lives, and I take my mind off that nightmare.

· 3 ·
A Nightmare Call

(APRIL 22, 2017)

....

"Baba, I miss you. Please pray for me!"

....

AS I PACE THE FLOOR from my office to the living room, that fore-warning—"He's leaving you for eternity"—engulfs me like a tidal wave from the ocean.

"Oh, NO! God!" I scream. "PLEASE, no! Oh, God, NO!"

Stop! You don't know what's happened. Hope!

I remember that once, as a toddler, Ethan filled the house with his bloodcurdling screams. Then Nathan, joined by Elesha, shouted, "Ethan poked his eye out! He poked his eye out!" Running into the lounge like a madman, I saw a flow of red oozing from his eye. But Ethan had merely tipped a bottle of undiluted raspberry drink into his eye, and he was terrified by his siblings' assessment of what had happened. I had imagined the worst, since I go crazy if I think my kids have hurt themselves. But my recollection does little to calm me nor my awareness that we had always averted a tragedy.

The sharp ring of the phone jolts me, and I feel the hardness of the wooden floor under my feet as I turn mid-stride and march into my office. I clench the phone and feel my clammy hands against the dry, plastic receiver.

"Mark Roser speaking!"

"Mr. Roser, this is Detective Uhlir with the Wheaton Police."

There's a long pause. I wait, pressing the phone against my ear.

"Your son was in an accident."

My chest tightens and my stomach knots. My knees press against the desk.

"He was hit during the hammer throw competition."

What's he talking about? *A hammer?* I thought he was in a car accident.

"It was rough. Are you sitting down?"

Oh, God! I gasp for air, and I slump into my seat.

"Yes," I mutter, trying to breathe and brace myself; yet, my insides are falling.

"Your son didn't make it to the hospital."

That is impossible. That can't be right!

"You're trying to tell me Ethan is dead?"

"I am very sorry."

I open my mouth to speak but no words will form. There's nothing more to say.

"Mr. Roser, are you still there?"

The best part of me is ripped away, and a dark, heavy shroud is zipped, airtight, all around me. I rally all the strength that is left in me to faintly whisper, "I'm going to say good-bye."

I lay the phone down. There's nothing I can do. Shockwaves of sorrow rush over me like the surging flood of a tsunami. They overwhelm me, and questions deep as the ocean swirl around me like tangling seaweed.

My son is too precious, too young, too full of life. How can he be dead?

In the bedroom, Pat sits on the edge of the bed with the phone to her ear, questioning someone with terror in her voice.

"You're saying Ethan was hit by a sixteen-pound metal weight?"

"It's Wheaton," she mouths to me with lips quivering and eyes panic-stricken.

"Is my son living?" Pat asks the person on the phone.

She doesn't know yet . . .

"But you just said, 'They resuscitated him.' I'm going to talk to my husband!"

She hangs up and looks at me, her eyes pleading for help.

"They took Ethan to the hospital. They, the guy, said he had no pulse," she stammers. "They—he—said, resuscitated him in the ambulance."

"He's dead." I hear myself say it. "I just got off the phone with the detective. They got his pulse back for a second, but he died on the way to the hospital."

It doesn't sound like me saying it and nothing in me wants to believe it.

"No!" Pat cries, shaking her head from side to side.

"No pulse!" Her hands cradle her rocking head. "Oh, Mark, Ethan had no pulse! Oh, Mark, our baby! What has happened?"

I sit on the edge of the bed and put my arm around her shoulders and cry.

Pat stops crying, turns to me and says, "Last week, I woke up at four a.m. in fear that Ethan would be in an accident. I kept telling myself—He's okay. He's already made the drive back to Chicago. I sent him a text at five a.m., saying, 'Hi, I'm up praying for you right now.' And now this. I just don't understand."

What do I say? Where do I start? Where do I end? If it were only some kind of bizarre mistake, a really sick joke—if it were anything but this—I could bear it. I could speak to it. Ethan had also texted me saying, "Baba, I miss you. Please pray for me!"

I pray for my Ethan every day by name, and God has always shielded him! In Psalm 91, he tells us not to fear the arrow that flies by day. "A thousand may fall at your side, and ten thousand at your right hand. But it shall not come near you!" He promised to give his angels charge over Ethan to keep him in all his ways, and to bear him up in their hands.

How can something like this happen? In America? *At a school?*

I grab some clothes, and stuff them in a small bag. I don't want to go to Chicago. I want my son brought back to me.

In the living room, I take my Bible off the windowsill and flip it open. My eyes fall on the words, "For He will finish the work and cut *it* short in righteousness. Because the LORD will make a short work upon the earth" (Romans 9:28).

Ethan's life cut short. I put the Bible down.

"But why, God?" I groan, and thoughts swirl that are all but audible: *Ethan would've served you for decades! It doesn't make sense to end his life. How can you let this happen? It's not right.*

While all around me an empty, chaotic void shouts, *He's dead! He's dead!*

In our entranceway, I lie prostrate on the floor. I've no words to pray, just silent tears that wet the wooden floor. My heart cries out for answers: *Could I have somehow prevented this? If I had prayed more or fasted? If I had made Ethan finish his year in Dallas?*

I loathe every silent, waiting second, each tick of the clock. Time has become a ravenous beast. But I'm powerless against it. As in an awful nightmare, my mind shouts, *Hurry, run! Do something.* But my feet are frozen. The monster pounces on me and splits me open, gnashing on me with its teeth. *Hurry—finish me off!* No! It watches me bleed.

My life is shattered. My world is ruined.

I lie on the floor for what seems an eternity.

"Oh, God," I finally manage the words. "I don't understand why you didn't prevent it! You've never hurt me like this. Why hurt me like this? Wasn't there another way?"

Pat meets me in the foyer as the sun rises the morning after Ethan died. She gets on her knees and looks into my eyes where I lie.

"We must go on," she says, "with our lives."

Her words hit me like a sledgehammer, and I begin weeping, loudly. Sorrow engulfs me like raging flood waters. My whole body shakes. Never have I cried like this. Never have I felt such despair. Never have I been so completely crushed.

Go on with our lives? What life? I don't even want to live. Not without Ethan. My heart, all my dreams for my son, for my family, for my world, lie fragmented, all around me, like a thousand shards of a broken windshield.

Unable to utter a word, I can't believe she is saying this—hours after our boy died. A burst of anger is unable to ignite. My broken heart can only feel anguish and sadness.

Must we go on with our lives? Maybe you can go on with your life. But I cannot!

At last, I get words out, "The only thing we must do is get to Chicago. Find out what happened."

· 4 ·

How Could This Happen?

"I don't know, but they must produce a lot of power."

NATHAN STOPS AT A RED LIGHT before the entrance ramp to the highway. He looks at me through his rear-view mirror. Our eyes meet. He's checking to see how I'm doing.

Last night, when we got to his apartment, he took one look at me. "What's wrong?" When I told him, he sobbed. Nathan was so protective of his little brother. They shared a room for twelve years. The day Nathan left for college, Ethan stood at the top of the basement steps, tears streaming down his face. Their lives were intertwined. Nathan and I had already blocked off the dates in the fall to watch Ethan play soccer at Wheaton.

Johnathan turns toward the backseat. "Do you know how it happened?" he asks me.

"No, we still need to find out."

"I'm getting lots of messages," Pat says. "I can feel the prayers."

My phone vibrates with another email of condolence. The news is spreading.

As we make our way north through Indiana, giant wind turbines, hundreds of feet tall, occupy the wide stretches of farmland on both sides of the highway as far as I can see. As if from another world, their long angelic arms reach heavenward, rotating effortlessly through the clouds. Shiny and white, they stand in tidy rows and spin at a steady pace.

Five months ago, Ethan and I admired these landmarks when we made this same drive. "How do they store energy?" I wondered out loud. "I don't know," Ethan replied, "but they must produce a lot of power."

Rubbing my neck and supporting my head with my hand, I lean against the door and re-read Ethan's last text message to me. "I have exams before we finish, but I plan to be home by May 14. I'm excited to see you. I love you Baba! I miss you. Please pray for me."

My response: "I pray for you every day and I will continue to pray for you. I love you sooo much!!!"

My phone rings—a Chicago area code.

"Hi, I'm Joe Mahr with *The Chicago Tribune*. I realize this is a very difficult time for you, but would you be willing to tell us about Ethan? From the people we've spoken with, he was an amazing young man."

His word—"was," in the past tense—pierces my heart, and I don't know where to start to tell him about Ethan. . . .

"Yeah, um, a really good kid, unusually secure, lots of friends. He brought us a lot of joy. Wow, I haven't been with him in a couple weeks," I ramble.

"I understand you are people of faith," he says.

"Yes, I've always believed things happen for a reason. But this is really hard to fathom."

With the wind and rumble on the highway, I strain to hear what he is saying to me.

"I have severe hearing loss," I pipe up. "Many ear infections as a child."

His voice rises, and he says, "I have plenty to write."

How I wish I could hear. I own hearing aids, but audiologists have explained why they don't help me. They recommended a cochlear implant. The kicker is that I've developed tinnitus, a buzzing, hissing, chirping, and whistling sound in my ears. It never stops. The background noise of highway driving at least helps mask these damaged, misfiring cochlear hairs. A highway conversation is, however, virtually impossible for me.

Pat, Nathan, and Johnathan are handling most of the calls. Nathan has just talked to CBS in New York City and Johnathan to NBC in Chicago. Setting his mobile down, "A reporter," Nathan says, "asked about the school's safety protocol. I told him: I'm not talking about that. But I'll tell you about Ethan and his faith."

Ethan's death is making national news: the unusualness of the accident, at a track and field event, killing a young man, the son of missionaries, an athletic ministry student, at a top Christian college. As a result, my family has opportunities to share our faith in Christ with several large media outlets. Yet, sharing my faith has never cost me so dearly. Talking about Jesus and heaven, when I hurt like hell, takes witnessing to a whole new dimension. When a family faces the tragic loss of a loved one, it's understandable that they want privacy. I told my family this morning, however, that we must honor God and Ethan. Maybe someone will be encouraged to look to God in their pain, and say to themselves, "If God can get them through that, he can get me through this." That is what I also told the last reporter who phoned me.

An hour later at Wheaton College, we enter an old building that looks like a fort. It's made of large, rough stone blocks and stands about four stories high. An American flag flies from a mount on the roof. We go up a flight of steps and through a reception area into a tidy carpeted office with bookshelves lining three walls. We sit in armchairs and on a sofa in a semi-circle in front of a solid wooden desk.

Elesha looks over at me with puffy, bloodshot eyes. She was in North Carolina yesterday at her roommate's wedding reception. What a horrifying contrast—I could hear laughter in the background—before I broke the news to her. I hated to have to tell her on the phone that her little brother was dead. She too hasn't slept, driving overnight to Cincinnati and flying to Chicago this morning.

The president of Wheaton College, Philip Ryken—brown hair, six feet tall, medium build, with black-rimmed glasses—takes a seat in front of the desk. Paul Chelsen, vice president of student development, shorter with lighter hair, takes a seat to his right.

"I'm not sure if you know how much your son was loved by the Wheaton community," Ryken says. "The campus is in mourning, and there's a Service of Lament at seven p.m. which we would like you to attend."

Ryken catches his breath. "I do need to tell you that the volunteers were told not to turn their backs to the field at any time. But from the reports I've received, Ethan had his back turned."

Too numb with pain, I say nothing, but his words hit me like a slap in the face. My family is also silent, and his words hang uneasily in the air. The silence is deafening.

A long moment later, Ryken asks, "What do you need to do while you're in Chicago?"

"Go to the coroner when they open tomorrow."

I hear myself say "coroner," and it drives home the dreadful reality. *Don't weep*, I urge myself, and I shift in my seat.

"We also need to meet with the police. I don't know what else we'll need to do," I say.

"You can meet with the police here on campus," Ryken replies.

"I'm not sure what the proper protocol is."

We'll go to the station, I tell myself.

"Could we go to the field where it happened?" I ask.

My family quickly nods in agreement.

"Certainly! I'll have our staff who were present when it happened join us there."

Ryken rises from his chair and leads us out of his office, and in the parking lot, my family piles back into Nathan's Yaris. Ryken and Chelsen get into an SUV.

Once we're moving, Johnathan says, "That doesn't sit well with me what he said about Ethan having his back turned. I think he's defending the school."

"They are good people," Pat says. "I don't want us to talk badly about them."

I keep quiet as the SUV parks in front of a house adjacent to an open field. To our right, the field lies in a rectangular shape and is surrounded by houses. Expecting a stadium, I'm taken aback by this simple green space in the middle of a modest suburb. The field has no track to run on, no fences, and no stands, just grass. It's more suited to throwing Frisbee, not sixteen-pound weights. We get out of the car. Johnathan's eyes meet mine: *Is this really it?*

On the street side of the field, a metal screen catches my attention. It's around twenty feet tall, has netting around it, and takes the shape of a horseshoe. I step onto the grass and notice chalk line markings. These start inside the area of the screen and fan outward some forty yards in the shape of a triangle, marking the field.

Two men and a woman are waiting for us near the cage. Ethan's soccer coach, Jake, the athletic director, and the track coach introduce themselves. Jake is about 5'10", forty years of age, with short dark hair, and razor stubble. My family gathers around them as do Ryken and Chelsen.

Ryken looks over at the Wheaton staff members as they explain what happened.

"Ethan was with three guys who had volunteered to measure and retrieve the hammer throws."

My head spins.

"It happened during the warm-ups."

I feel lightheaded and faint; the earth beneath me is giving way. . . .

"The volunteers were told to never turn their heads from the cage."

"Do you make an announcement," I exclaim, "a whistle, a flag, or something to let them know, before these hammers are thrown in the air?"

"No," the track coach says, looking over at me. "The NCAA doesn't require that."

"Did any of the other boys have their backs turned?" I ask.

"One of the guys was on his way from returning a hammer, heard it whiz over his head, and saw Ethan turn toward the field just before it hit him."

Whiz over his head . . . saw Ethan . . . Doesn't that mean this guy also had his back turned?

"What did the third boy see?" I ask, as a million questions scream at me.

"He fell down to get out of the way, but it ricocheted off Ethan and grazed him slightly."

I glance at Ryken. It barely misses a boy and hits another. *How can it be Ethan's fault?* This doesn't make sense. It could've killed any of them.

"Who was watching these boys?" I ask. "Where was the closest supervisor?"

Ryken looks at the coaches for an answer.

"I was at a nearby field," the head track and field coach says, "but the event coach and Coach Jake were here."

"I was fifty yards away. I shouted, 'Watch out!' Then I saw it hit Ethan, and I came running."

While my mind spins faster, trying to process what I'm hearing, Pat asks, "Did he struggle?"

"No! He fell down and didn't move. I was the first one to get to him," Coach Jake says. "He had no pulse." Coach Jake looks like he's going to cry.

"They made a valiant effort," Ryken exclaims. "Did CPR, everything they could. Police and paramedics arrived immediately."

"How many people saw my son die?" Pat asks.

"There were about a hundred people. Members of the Wheaton track team got on their knees to pray, and all the other athletes from the other schools were also on their knees."

"Where," I ask, fighting back my urge to weep, "was Ethan standing?"

"Over there," Coach Jake points left outside the chalk markings.

There's a pile of sand where he points about forty yards from us, a wheelbarrow's worth of sand, spread heavily on the grass. *Oh, God, he must've bled a whole lot.* That sand marks the exact spot Ethan died.

My family instinctively takes a step in the direction of the pile of sand.

"Could you please," Elesha's voice rises to a stern pitch, "give us a moment alone?"

Ryken immediately steps back and the Wheaton staff retreat toward their cars with him. My family and I turn and walk slowly in the direction of the pile of sand.

Approaching it, I look down and see the red of Ethan's blood clotted with the sand. He took his last breath here only a few hours ago. His life blood poured out of him upon the ground where we stand.

My knees give way and I slump down to the ground. All my strength is gone; his life was spilled like water, squandered like dirt.

What wrong did he do? Feelings of anger attempt to form in my heart. *How could he die here?* This is not supposed to happen. *Why didn't God take me instead?* Ethan had his whole life to live!

Pat, Johnathan, Elesha, and Nathan get on their knees beside me. The sound of them crying, the question of why, the brutality of it—and a soft breeze blows across the bloody, motionless sand.

"My son, it wasn't your fault," I whisper. "You mustn't bear the blame."

Weeping, Johnathan takes some of the sand in his hand and rubs it between his fingers.

If we could go back through the hours, gather Ethan's life up, separate the grains of sand from his precious blood, we would make our stand here. Together, we would live and not die. If we had been with him, it never would have happened!

"Oh, God!" I get the words out. "Please help us!"

My mind goes blank while my family prays.

The next thing I know, we're walking back across Lawson Field toward where the school officials wait for us. Two young women and a young man approach us before we cross the street.

They must be students.

One of the women hands Pat a bouquet of yellow and purple flowers. She then looks at me, eyes big and sad, and she says softly, "We're so sorry."

· 5 ·

Ethan's Last Days

....

"Love is dependent on our ability to choose."

....

MEETING US AS WE CROSS THE STREET, Chelsen hands me a single key. "Here's the key to Ethan's room," he says. "His roommate has moved out."

No doubt, it's too painful for Kyle to be in that room with Ethan gone. "Ethan Roser / Kyle Shoemaker"—their names are handwritten on the door.

I helped Ethan move into his room four months ago. Taking a deep breath, I turn the key and swing the door open. My family warily follows me into the last place Ethan lived—hours ago.

No more laughter, no more studies, no more play, no more sleep for our boy here. Silence, stillness, and sadness pervade the room.

Side by side, American and Zimbabwean flags hang proudly, covering the longest wall. On Ethan's table his books and papers rest where he left them. His familiar backpack hangs on his chair, the top unzipped with a white and black folder hanging out. The netted compartment of his backpack is filled with gospel tracts, rubber-banded together, and two pocket-sized copies of John's Gospel.

From the closet, Ethan's clothes stare at me—never to adorn him again. On the floor, his shoes, an assortment of Toms and his leather Sperry loafers, all wait for his feet in vain. Ethan's fondness for shoes once amused me, but now it hurts to look at them.

I sigh when I locate Ethan's soccer uniform. It questions me. *Where has he gone?*

How often he wore you, my thoughts call back. How many places we went for games, hotels, and meals out. How many conversations we had during the long miles driving to tournaments. And how well we got to know and love each other.

Breaking the silence, Pat says, "All I could think about was get me to his room, let me find the scent of my son one more time. For years I did his laundry and tried to rid his clothes of that pungent odor of sweat. But there's so little smell of Ethan here."

She picks up her boy's pillow and cuddles it in her arms. She breathes deeply to smell her boy's scent one last time. Tenderly, she presses it against her face and weeps into it.

Johnathan, Elesha, and Nathan look stunned. It's too much for me. I hear myself whimper. We put our arms around Pat and cry aloud. I can't believe he is gone.

A lump in my throat forms, and I swallow hard as I take an inventory of my son's things: a Liverpool soccer poster, the picture of an old fisherman sitting in a boat smoking a pipe, the wooden wheel of a ship, a boat compass, his family album, and a shoe box of keepsakes. Everything in the room speaks of him in sacred tones. Ethan didn't own much in his life. He was content with so little. He was just starting to make a life for himself. He should've had more.

Tapping me on the shoulder, Nathan says, "Ethan wrote a paper. It is titled, 'Why Evil Exists.' It's like he left us a message."

"It's the only paper out on his desk," Johnathan adds, as Nathan hands it to me.

> Why is there evil in a world created by a good and all-powerful God? The answer begins with free will, in which God gives Man the ability to accept or reject His love. God created Man with free will, because He desires an authentic relationship. Free will ensures an authentic relationship, because love is dependent on our ability to choose. If Man could not choose whether to love God or not, then Man would be merely a robot-like reflex. . . .

A knock on the door.

"Ethan's car keys," a guy says, handing them to me.

We are invited to meet with Ethan's friends in the student lounge, and the soccer team at Coach Jake's house. Two hours pass. We talk to more media outlets, and then we drive to Pierce Chapel on the Wheaton College campus for the seven p.m. Service of Lament.

We're met by school staff in the parking lot.

But I don't want to be here. I want to go back to the hotel and sleep. I'm wrecked. I'm done. I'm frazzled and conflicted!

College should be a safe place. But it was an unforeseeable accident. No, it could've been prevented! It's nobody's fault. Then why blame Ethan? He should have been more alert. No, they should have supervised him better! Back and forth my thoughts go. . . .

We are promptly ushered into a side entrance, and I hear faint melodious singing. We're led through a second door, which takes us into the front of a spacious chapel. We're shown seats but remain standing, along with 1,000 students. From the young solemn faces, I turn to the empty stage. Where's the source of the soothing music? Then I see two guitarists and a vocalist sitting at floor level below the stage. Their harmonious voices sound angelic.

In the balcony more students are crowded, shoulder to shoulder, singing. To my right, I recognize the Wheaton soccer players that we met at Coach Jake's house. They occupy the entire first two pews. Earlier today, they had filled Coach Jake's house. It was like a military funeral for a fallen comrade. A player wept and told us in a trembling voice, "At first, I wasn't interested in getting to know Ethan. I thought he might take my spot on the team. But Ethan befriended me, and the morning he died, he said to me, 'I want God to use me to reach the world for Christ.' Now it's happening," he said with tears. "CNN, ESPN, and every news outlet are telling of his love for Christ and others." Afterward, he told us that he would have been on the field if Ethan had not taken his place, and that before he met Ethan, he had identity issues, suffered from severe depression, and did not want to live. But Ethan's love for God and others, as he and Ethan often talked about Jesus, turned his life completely around.

As we sing, I try to focus on the words projected on the screen, and an older man approaches me and gently places his hand on my shoulder. "Would it be all right," he asks, "If the students gather around you and pray for your family?"

"Yes, that would be fine," and I nod my head. It feels like everything is in slow motion.

Another surge of grief, a piercing sorrow stabs me in the pit of my stomach. It's unlike anything I've ever known. I had grieved my dad's death. We were close. He handled all our mission stuff, stateside, and we traveled together to churches. But this is different. My dad was old. Ethan was young. I anticipated my dad's demise, but Ethan's death was unimaginable. My dad's body wore out, but Ethan was strong and vibrant.

How can I accept this? How can I give up my son?

"I want you to know how special Ethan was to me and our team," Coach Jake told us earlier today. "Your son was a wonderfully complex combination of a man: on one hand, he was gentle, thoughtful, and caring, a brilliant listener who was extremely teachable. On the other hand, he was tough, persistent, and disciplined."

Waves of grief hit me, and all that I heard today roars around me like sprays of the sea.

"My wife and I recently lost our fourth child midway through her pregnancy," Coach Jake had also said. "I was devastated and sent out an email. Ethan wrote me back within minutes. Then he followed up with a handwritten card. I was surprised, not because other players hadn't reached out to me, too, but because of the depth of compassion in Ethan's words."

Coach Jake had handed Ethan's card to Pat, and later she gave it to me. I re-read what Ethan wrote: "Coach, God is amidst the pain and the suffering. He walks with us in the most troubling times. I'm continually praying for you and your wife. Psalm 116 says 'The cords of death entangled me. The anguish of the grave came over me. I was overcome by stress and sorrow. Then I called on the name of the Lord—'Lord save me.'"

A man stands at a lectern and reads from the Bible. I can't hear what he says. My ears are like burned toast, and my brain like scrambled eggs.

Pens and slips of paper are placed along the platform from left to right. Students come to the front. They take the pens in hand and the slips of beige paper. They lean against the stage and write. More and more students crowd the stage, two rows deep, thoughtfully writing on the slips of paper. I'm puzzled. My mind is clocking out.

"Dad," Elesha whispers in my ear, "they're writing notes to give us."

Yes, I know everyone wants to comfort us. The students are so kind. But my soul refuses to be comforted. A sword has entered my heart. My wound is too deep. I want my son back! Nothing else will do. . . .

Another tap on the shoulder: Jeremiah, Ethan's friend whom we met earlier in the dorm lounge, has three kids with him.

"They're from the Young Life group at Glen Ellyn that Ethan and I did," he says.

They each give me a hug.

Jeremiah told us earlier in the student lounge, "I was self-conscious, but Ethan brought me out of myself. He walked up to people in downtown Chicago and asked, 'Would you like to talk about Jesus?' Ethan was playful but also intense. He was unique that way. Ethan told me, 'We need to get this stuff down. We've got to understand what we're being taught while we have time.' Plain and simple," Jeremiah told us, "your son changed my life."

Minutes pass as the students leave the slips of paper on the stage and return to their seats.

"When Ethan first arrived at Wheaton," another friend of Ethan told us, "he was so excited to meet people that he rode the Fischer elevator up and down, stopping at every floor to say 'Hi' to whoever he saw. He also gave free haircuts to whoever wanted one."

Ethan as a small boy—I see him—sitting in the kitchen, allowing me to cut his hair. He loved using our electric clippers—I knew it was an honor of trust when he let me cut his hair.

My legs beg me to sit. At last, everyone takes their seats again, and I plop into mine.

Then I hear Pat's voice. . . .

Oh, wow, she's at the lectern. I hear her say Ethan's name. She's energetic and courageous. She talks for about five minutes and then motions in our direction.

"Mom wants you to go up and speak," Elesha says.

I don't want to speak and say the wrong thing. But Elesha nudges me, and I get on my feet. Slowly, I drag my body across the front of the chapel to the lectern. What can I say to these young, precious lives, still being formed? They all willingly came to lament our loss. I must comfort them.

"A week ago—ah, it was before Ethan died, I read . . . read from Isaiah chapter 57. Here's my paraphrase: 'The righteous perish and no one ponders it . . . in his heart. Devout men are taken away, and no one . . . no one seems to care.' But tonight, you've taken our son's death to heart."

My voice is breaking up. "You've . . . embraced our pain . . . as though it were your own. You've deeply touched our hearts. . . ."

My voice abandons me. "Thank you," I gabble, and quickly head for my seat.

Nathan and Pat follow me back to our seats, and another man stands at the lectern. I don't catch what he says, but he motions in our direction with his hand.

The soccer team files out of their two rows, and they come over to me and my family. Then, students start coming from all over the chapel, and there is a crowd all around us.

Some kneel. Others stand. Some lay their hands on me, others on my family. Bodies, hands, mouths, a throng surrounds the five of us. In earnest, they all begin praying at the same time, some with moans and cries. I can't hear much of what they pray, but I feel the warmth and intensity of their intercession for us. The long pleadings eventually end; hugs begin. The love is heartfelt and tangible. . . . But I am kaput.

An hour later we're in our hotel room at the Hyatt Regency in Lisle. I'm in bed with Pat. The lights are off. Johnathan and Elesha are asleep in a double next to us. Nathan sleeps on the pullout sofa across the room.

Ethan was with us the last time we were in Chicago; we all shared a similar room. The rest of the family joined Ethan and me to watch the Reds play the Cubs at Wrigley Field. He had learned to enjoy baseball as I'd learned to enjoy soccer. But Ethan knew baseball was my favorite and used to tease me, saying, "Dad, I'm going to have a T-shirt made for you. It'll say, 'If it was easy, it'd be called baseball.'"

But now hurtful thoughts—nothing will ever be the same. Ethan will never again be with us! We will never again be a complete family! These thoughts invade my mind the way rebels invade a city whose walls are breached. He'll never sleep in his bed again. Never! Each thought stabs my heart, but I mustn't cry and wake my family.

My bed, ever a place of comfort, has become a place of absolute torment. My heart is screaming bloody murder.

Ethan will never read that book you got him, which sits on your desk: *I Am Not But I Know I Am.* Oh, how I looked forward to giving my son that book and discussing it with him this summer. God's name, "I am that I am," fascinated Ethan, and I had to get him Louis Giglio's latest book.

Ethan wanted those Hebrew letters—I AM THAT I AM—tattooed above his heart, but he was seventeen, and a tattoo required my consent. He showed me verses in the Bible where God's name was written on his people. So, I wrote the Hebrew letters on his chest with a black marker, so he could see exactly what they looked like for a couple of days.

"I like it," he said. "I'll use it to share Christ!"

"Let's wait ninety days," I suggested, and while waiting, he found a Christian tattoo guy in Columbus. I'll never forget his face the day he was tattooed. He looked like he'd really gotten away with something. His older siblings were shocked that I had signed off on it. Under the old regime, which they grew up under, they wouldn't have even asked for a tattoo! How I had mellowed by the time Ethan was born.

But now, he'll never ask you questions about God—tormenting thoughts persist. He'll never offer you an answer.

Last year, we'd both read and discussed J. I. Packer's classic, *Knowing God.* His answers always fascinated me—his thoughts were so unique and fresh. When he became our only child at home, I poured myself, my time and energy, into him.

· 6 ·

A Similar Question

....

*"Studying theology feels like I'm trying to
empty the ocean with a teaspoon."*
*"I love my Young Life team. I love Jesus.
This is about to be so much fun."*

....

I WAKE UP . . . I've slept! The clock on the nightstand says 2:54 a.m. My
first two hours of sleep since Ethan passed, and now I'm wide awake.

I need to respond to my emails.

Quietly, I get out of bed and grab my clothes. I slip out of our room,
catching the door before it bangs, and ride the elevator to an empty
hotel lobby.

The receptionist appears, walking with a slight limp.

"What happened to your leg?" I ask, as I sit in a black leather chair.

"I was born with a shorter leg. I've had many surgeries."

"That's hard!"

He takes a seat across from me. "I heard about your son from the
day manager. We're all really sorry." He looks into my eyes. "You're a
missionary."

"Yes. We spent twenty-two years in Africa."

"My younger sister was raped in our house."

I can see he wants to talk.

"That's terrible," I say. "Must've been really hard for her."

"It almost destroyed our family. I've often wondered," he says, "why it happened."

"Today, I found a paper my son wrote on 'Why Evil Exists.' He pointed out how God gave us the power to choose, and without that ability love is impossible."

"But my sister didn't choose to be raped. She didn't even know the guy who raped her."

"What I mean is that 'free will' made evil and rape a possibility. Cain chose to murder Abel. At times, we suffer because of the sins of others. But free will also makes love, which is the greatest good, possible. Otherwise, we would be what Ethan called 'a robot-like reflex,' and 'an authentic relationship' with God would be nonexistent. More like animals or even endowed with less—like nature's laws at work."

In an instant, my own theological studies come to mind: evil started with Lucifer, a bright, beautiful angel created with a free will who became proud and chose to misuse his great gifts, forming his own kingdom, which became the antithesis of all the good God created. Humankind chose to follow Satan's rebellion, and evil entered our world: moral evils like rape, as well as natural disasters, like tornadoes, and every tragic accident like Ethan's.

"You mean God just watches people, and they can do whatever they choose to do?"

"No. God is active in our world. It may not look like it, but he is not a passive spectator. Amid the choices people make, God acts and he decides the outcome. Our choices are limited. But how he does that while we are free to act is hard for us to comprehend with our finite minds. But God is infinite in his power and ways."

"So, God can stop things from happening?"

"Yes, he can. Often, God restrains people from doing what they want. He gave us a conscience, and I would bet God's Spirit also dealt with that man about his evil desires many times before that day. . . ."

"But why," the receptionist interrupts, "does God sometimes stop things from happening and other times he doesn't?"

"Well, if God intervened every time, our free will would be compromised, and we could not develop our own character."

"It doesn't seem fair that God allows somebody's evil choices to ruin somebody else's life."

"We can also choose how we respond to someone who hurts us. God can also somehow make it up to us."

"Does God only intervene through people's consciences?"

"No. God can intervene in other ways too. Somebody could've come home before your sister was raped. . . ."

"IF I had been there, I would have hurt that guy bad. Hey, wouldn't God expect me to do everything I can to stop my sister from being raped? So, why didn't he do something to stop it?"

"God promises to soon stop all evil, and he will more than hurt evildoers. There is a second death in a lake of fire."

"I'd rather think that he couldn't stop it because he gave us free will. That makes more sense to me."

In *God's Sovereignty*, I wrote that if there was even one thing outside God's control, we would need to fend for ourselves in that thing, and not depend on him. God rules over not just the big picture but the smallest details. His providence directs all contingencies, even the apparent chance of our rolling dice or a sparrow falling to the ground or where a hammer throw lands. I've often preached these things to others.

But now I see that steel weight hit Ethan, and I wonder—did God limit himself? Was he hampered from stopping the receptionist's sister from being raped or my son from being killed because he gave us a free will? The biblical doctrine of God's sovereignty is a double-edged sword. It can comfort and assure us. But it can also alarm and cut us.

Don't worry. God is still on the throne, ruling. Then why am I suffering? What wrong have I done?

"Some people believe God can't stop things because of free will, but in the Bible, we see that God is very active in people's lives and he is sovereign over all things. You see, God really wants us to trust him, and how can we trust God if he's not Almighty? Better not to jump if our Father can't catch us. And his 'hands off approach' would mean that everything in life depends on us and others, not him."

"Yeah, but how can I trust a God who can stop my sister from being raped and chooses not to? I mean he expects you and me to behave in a consistent manner! Why doesn't he? Why should I trust him?"

"That is a good question, and the Bible has a good answer. We can trust God because he demonstrated his steadfast love by sending Jesus to die on the cross for our sins. Christ defeated Satan and delivered us from his domain and our fear of evildoers. Christ brings us to God in a way that we freely love him. That love for God enables us to trust him no matter what, but our love will be tested."

I'm preaching to myself now, and it's far easier to preach this than to live it.

"Why," he softly asks, "do you think God allowed my sister to be raped?"

"I don't know," I tenderly say.

I believe God has his reasons, but what do we do if God doesn't catch us and we hit the ground?

An older man enters the lobby and looks at the reception desk.

The young man stands and excuses himself, walking with a limp over to his station.

I once thought it wasn't good to ask the "why" question. But questions are inevitable.

There were a thousand things God could've done to prevent Ethan from being hit by that hammer, and this young guy has thought a lot about why God allowed his sister to be raped. Faith does not leave our questions unanswered. The Bible says, "by faith, we understand," and without faith we cannot understand how the world got here, why we are here, or if there is anything beyond death (Hebrews 11:3).

From my laptop bag, I take out notes that I was given last night at the Service of Lament.

Rilea: "Ethan asked me if he could tell me a funny story. 'You know that evangelism class I've been taking? Well, I wasn't properly registered for it.' He said it with his dumbfounded grin, devoid of any bitterness. When Ethan calmly told me he wasn't registered, I had thought, if that were me, I'd be freaking out until I got credit for all my class work."

Max: "I went downtown with Ethan to share Jesus. We talked with several people and I was sitting on a bench, but Ethan was determined to share with one more guy. In the Bible, I imagine that Stephen's death was surrounded by a similar question of 'Why, God?' God clarified 'why,' and it led to the spread of the gospel. My prayer for Ethan's death is that it would be clarified and have even greater ramifications for our faith than Stephen's death. This is an audacious prayer, but we are connected to the God of miracles."

Max raises the same question I have, but his request is far more audacious than mine.

Just then, sunlight appears in the entrance windows, and the receptionist walks over to me and says, "The day manager just came on duty. He wanted you to have these," and he hands me five complimentary breakfast vouchers. "I would've liked to talk more, but I've got to work."

"You have very good questions," I reply.

He returns to the reception desk, and I remember a conversation I had years ago with a librarian at Hebrew Union College in Cincinnati.

"How can you believe in an all-good and all-powerful God considering the Holocaust?" she asked me.

"God has an answer to all our questions," I said. "The Jewish prophets dedicated entire books to explain 'why' things like the destruction of the temple and the Babylonian captivity happened. Have you ever asked God?"

"I'm asking you!" the librarian said. "I don't believe he exists."

"Have you ever read the book of Job?" I asked.

"Not lately," she replied.

"Job was an upright man who lost all his children, and he feels God has been unjust with him. His complaint develops into a lawsuit, if you will, to arraign God over his mistreatment. God answers Job with a critical piece of information: Job is involved in a cosmic conflict against wicked spirits in high places. Satan, God's arch-enemy and the accuser of men, is having a go at him."

Then, I told her plainly, "The devil hates the Jewish people because God brought his word and his Son into the world through Abraham's descendants. The promised seed was destined to crush the serpent. We are involved in a life-and-death struggle between good and evil."

"If I don't believe in God," she said, "why would I believe in the devil?"

"It sounds like you do. Without God, there is no absolute basis for good or evil. Not even the Holocaust is evil in an objective sense. If God doesn't exist, we are here by mere chance and time. Then, the fact that people kill and pillage is simply the survival of the fittest. It may be bad for one group or the other. But to say it is evil? Who decides? The masses? Government? Each individual? We have seen where those answers lead. Here is the problem with using the existence of evil to deny God's existence: we all have an innate sense of good and evil. Where did we get that from? Our conscience is evidence for God. Our appreciation of goodness and beauty helps us to be aware of when we have fallen away from what is good."

I'll never forget that conversation. . . .

Now with Ethan gone, I imagine I'd answer her better than I did then. I would tell her God "does not afflict willingly [literally from the heart], Nor grieve the children of men" (Lamentations 3:33). Nor is he "willing that any should perish but that all should come to repentance" (2 Peter 3:9). I would tell her about my pain, and my question for God. I would tell her that what happened to the receptionist's sister and to her people in the Holocaust was not from God's hand but the devil's (Job 2:6).

Evil acts expose the stark contrast between what theologians call God's permissive will and his perfect will. Permissive, because when God permits or allows things, he has chosen *not* to act to prevent them from happening. But choosing not to act is also an act of the will. God is not a control freak. He allows people to make real choices, and, at times, hurtful choices, even blaspheming his name, deliberately disobeying his laws, persecuting his saints, even rejecting his Son. He allows things he hates. Things I hate!

Boy, the devil must hate me.

Was Satan granted permission to kill my son to test me like Job or sift me like wheat as he did Peter? (Job 2:13; Luke 22:31). I know Satan cannot do whatever he wants. I'm sure he didn't appreciate my book *The Cleansing of the Heavens*. In it, I expounded on Satan's main modus operandi as the accuser who seeks grounds to afflict us. The Bible compares him to a strongman, fully armed, who stands in God's presence as a prosecuting attorney, asking permission to cross-examine us and tempt us (Revelation 12:10; Zechariah 3:1). But didn't Jesus defeat and disarm the devil? (John 12:23–33; Colossians 2:14–15). Surely, he did; yet, the devil still goes about like a roaring lion, causing hurt and wreaking havoc (1 Peter 5:8; Revelation 12:9–13, 17). I can understand Satan hurting us when we don't submit to God or when we give him a place to operate in our lives through our sin (Ephesians 4:27; 6:11–20).

But where did I miss it?

It's gotten personal now and painful as hell. Nothing has ever devastated me like that steel device targeting Ethan.

It's almost six a.m. and I glance at my vouchers.

I'll wait for the restaurant to open for breakfast. I can answer text messages from my extended family. I can copy and paste the information I got as they all ask similar questions: *how did it happen?* But the story I've been given only adds to my heartache.

I can't tell them that Ethan was blamed.

And I've got no answer to the ultimate question: *Why did God allow it?* Am I suffering like Job? Or did Ethan or I open the door to Satan? I know that what God allows he allows for a reason. God must have had a good reason to permit Ethan's death. I ask why, not that I deny God's sovereign right to do with Ethan and me whatever He wills, but I ask God to tell me his reason because I seek to understand his purpose and cooperate with his will. I ask because I'm in a covenant relationship with him. I ask because I need something more than Augustine's or C. S. Lewis's theodicy. I ask for more than a generic answer. I ask for something specific. I ask because God is big enough to handle my question. Also, I ask because I believe in God's willingness and ability to communicate with me.

Just as Max prayed, I'll continue to ask God to tell me the reason for Ethan's death. But how could it have "greater ramifications for our faith" than Stephen's death? That is hard to imagine.

· 7 ·

Ethan's Precious Body

....

"Death never really bothered me."

....

AS THE SUN'S RAYS LENGTHEN THEIR ADVANCE toward me, I move into the breakfast area that has just opened for the day. Chewing slices of cantaloupe and sipping hot tea, I mull over the fact that last Sunday was Easter, and Jesus raised Lazarus from the dead a week before the first Easter. What a sign it would be if Jesus raised Ethan from the dead the week after this past Easter. Lazarus was dead four days. Ethan has been dead only two days, half that time. *Imagine the news: Multitudes turn to Christ.* Ethan and I would go everywhere, preaching! Christ would be glorified, and Ethan would be restored to me. Satan would be shamed, and everything would make sense.

Almighty God is a miracle worker. Nothing is too difficult for him. . . .

Looking up from the breakfast table, I'm surprised to see Pat and Elesha.

Keep those thoughts to yourself about God raising Ethan from the dead. I stand and pull out two chairs.

"When Johnathan and Nathan are up, we'll go to the morgue," I say, handing them each a voucher. "Get some breakfast."

Pat hands me a paper and says, "I grabbed Ethan's school papers from his backpack. You need to read this."

"Weekly Evangelism Report" is typed at the top of the page. Below it is the question, "How did the conversation begin?"

Ethan (3/31/17): "My friend asked me if I would talk to Calle over the phone about Jesus. I learned how scary death must be to people that don't know Jesus. Being a Christian my whole life, death never really bothered me. In many ways I almost look forward to it because it means I get to go to heaven. But hearing her fears and anxiety toward death helped me to share the hope we can have in Christ as I talked to her about death, heaven and anxiety."

Pat and Elesha return to the table with bowls of fruit and flaky croissants.

"Wow," I say, "less than a month ago, Ethan said, 'Death never really bothered me.' "

Johnathan joins us at the table. I hand him a voucher, and he hands me a piece of paper saying, "This note was given to me last night at the service. You need to read it."

The note reads, "Minutes after Ethan left this world, I gathered with students to pray. One of them saw Jesus come into the prayer room. Another student reported earlier that he saw Jesus on campus. I'm convinced that the Lord came to receive Ethan's spirit when he died."

What a remarkable claim—Jesus personally ushered Ethan into heaven. If true, that would be no small comfort, but my heart refuses to let go of my son and accept that he is gone.

Thirty minutes later, we are in the car together and headed to the morgue.

"DuPage County Coroner must be nearby," Nathan says, as he turns into a large parking lot and parks in one of the many open spaces.

We get out of his car and look around. An adjacent building has loading docks, and on the opposite side of the street are various commercial buildings. Nathan and I walk toward the sidewalk, looking for addresses. Johnathan, Pat, and Elesha walk a few steps behind us.

"I'll call them," Nathan says. "I'll find out which building it is."

Nathan talks to someone on his mobile. Then, he stops and turns toward to me.

"The guy on the phone said, 'Families don't come here, but since you're outside you may as well come in.'" Nathan then points. "It's that building over there."

We cross the street to a two-story building and enter through a set of glass doors. The man behind the counter, "Charlie Dastych, Chief Deputy Coroner," shows us a conference room off the reception area, and we sit at a long wooden table.

"We are very sorry for your loss," he says. "What a tragic accident." With a yellow legal pad and a pen in his hand, he looks around the table and asks, "What are your children's names?"

"Johnathan, Elesha, and Nathan." I recite their names.

The coroner writes their names, and he looks at Pat, saying, "and Ethan."

"Yes, Ethan is our fourth child," she says.

Saying our children's names and hearing Pat say, "Ethan is our fourth child," evokes an eerie sense of déjà vu. I think of when I said their names, counting them as I awoke, knowing we had four kids, not three. How strange that was, and when I was fully conscious, I wondered—*What is going on?*

I blurt out, "Could we be with Ethan?"

"In all my years," the coroner says, his eyebrows rising, "that doesn't go well for the family. The funeral home will prepare his body for you to view."

"We don't plan to have a visitation."

My mind searches for an appeal.

"My family lived in Africa for twenty-two years." My heart beats faster. "Family members were always with their loved ones right after they died. That became a part of our culture."

The coroner glances around the table at the rest of my family.

I can't let them dissect him or drain his blood.

"You can put a blanket over him," I say.

"Let me see what I can do," the coroner says, and he gets up and leaves the room.

"Dad," Elesha says, "don't do it!" There is panic in her voice.

"I don't think it's a good idea," Pat says.

Johnathan and Nathan are also shaking their heads, *No!*

"It'll just be me. I really need to do this."

My family can see that I'm determined.

"Dad, I'll go with you," Johnathan says.

"I will too," Nathan says.

The coroner comes back ten minutes later.

"This isn't what we normally do." He remains standing. "But we've moved Ethan to a room for you to visit with him for a moment."

Johnathan, Nathan, and I follow the coroner down a set of steps and around a corner into a hallway. We stop at a room on our left. It has a metal door with a glass window.

"I'll wait for you out here," the coroner says, and he swings the door open for us to enter the room where they have moved Ethan.

The walls are tiled. The floor is hard concrete. The room smells antiseptic like a hospital, but there is less light. The room is empty except for a table on wheels, positioned in the center of the room. Ethan lies on the table. A dark blanket covers him. But I can see the form of his head, the outline of his torso, and his feet protruding. My beloved is lifeless.

"My beautiful boy," I whisper. "What has happened to you?"

I move around the table to the far side of the room, while Johnathan and Nathan stand on the other side of the table near the door.

"I would never leave you here."

A terrible longing to hold my boy grips me. To remove the blanket, to look on his face, to peer into his eyes, to take him off the table, to somehow awaken him.

Reaching down, I gently touch Ethan's feet. I want to rub his muscular calf. That's how I would wake him on early mornings when we needed to travel for a soccer game. That's how I would get him up and out the door.

Oh, I must take you home with me!

He should not be here. This place is not meant for him. This is all a mistake. Taking a deep breath, I look again at the form of his body, from his head to his feet—from my body, very flesh of my flesh, my life's successor lies.

"Why, my son?" I ask under my breath. "Why have you left me?"

The room is cold. Yet, I feel sweat on the palms of my hands and under my shirt. I am suddenly lightheaded.

"Oh, God . . ."

I must ask!

"If it would please you, please bring Ethan back to life for your Son's glory."

I move around to the head of the table and touch Ethan's shoulder. I feel his body under the blanket as I press my hand down.

"Lord, nothing is impossible for you. Just say the word!"

When I say, "Just say the word," those dreadful words from my dream invade my thoughts and haunt me—"He's leaving you for eternity."

My heart sinks. I don't know what to pray. I'm out of breath. All my confidence is gone. . . .

"Thank you, God," I hear Johnathan say. "Thank you for Ethan. Thank you for the beautiful life he lived. Thank you that his soul is secure with you."

"Thank you," Nathan says, "that Ethan knew your Son, Jesus."

A long, quiet moment passes.

Our time has ended. We must go from here. Do the unthinkable. Leave Ethan: young, energetic, full of life, so many dreams, unfulfilled, lying in this cold morgue, this place of untimely death, this unbearable contradiction. I am powerless to do anything else.

We rejoin Pat and Elesha back upstairs. Before we leave the building, I say to the coroner, "Please accept these flowers as a token of our appreciation," and Elesha hands him the bouquet of yellow and purple flowers that the students gave us yesterday at Lawson Field.

Thirty minutes later, Nathan turns into the parking lot of Aero Removals, a low red brick building. At the entrance, the owner meets us. Frank Vosicky is heavyset, with a round face, head completely shaved, a trimmed gray mustache and goatee.

He leads us to an oval table, surrounded by high-back chairs with blue fabric.

"The coroner's office just phoned me," he says. "They'll have your son here tomorrow, and I can have him in Cincinnati on Wednesday."

"That will work. We're planning a memorial service for the weekend," I say. "Ethan has a lot of friends who are in school all week."

"You'll be amazed," Frank says, "at what we're able to do for your son's visitation."

"Ah, we don't plan on an open casket." Nobody could do Ethan justice. "We just want to remember him the way he looked before the accident."

There is a long pause, and he says, "All right, well, I'll still need you to sign these papers to have him embalmed. He can't leave the state of Illinois until he is embalmed."

Frank pulls a document out of a file. I sign it and pass it back to him.

He slides it across the table for Pat to sign. She touches it, and her face reddens. Abruptly, she gasps, and sobs erupt, bursting forth from within her. She places her head on the table, her body trembling, and her loud wailing fills the office.

Stunned, I move around the table and place my arms around her. I've never seen her cry this hard. Long minutes pass, and slowly, Pat takes the pen in her shaking hand. She signs her name, but the stark lines don't look like her signature.

In the parking lot, Pat says, "The finality of it walloped me. A mother gives life to her child. Then for me to sign papers so that they can do that to Ethan. It was just too much!"

Her weeping affects me more than all her strength. How can I be strong for her when I'm shattered? How can I help her when I don't understand why this has happened?

· 8 ·

An Empty Chair

....

ETHAN, GRADE FOUR, WESTERN ROW ELEMENTARY:
"I am from memories rooted in love.
I am from brown eyes and black hair. I am from Pat and Mark."

....

IT'S LATER THAN LUNCH AND EARLIER THAN DINNER, but we're hungry and stop to eat. We're the only customers in the restaurant. We order drinks, and a family enters—a mom and dad, a preteen boy, a younger girl, and a toddler. They're talking and happy. We're all quiet. We've lost our baby. Ethan's siblings are much older than he was, and he was their baby too; they gave him his bottle and got him out of his crib, watched him take his first steps, and read him stories at bedtime. As a waiter places our drinks on the table, I long to be the happy family sitting at a table on the other side of the restaurant.

Still looking over at the family, Pat says, "For thirty-three years, I've been learning how to be a better parent. My parents divorced when I was three, so I had a lot to learn. I think your dad and I made fewer mistakes with Ethan, but I want you to know how much we love each of you."

"We know that," Elesha says, and Johnathan and Nathan nod their heads.

We were forty when Ethan was born and more like grandparents in our child-rearing, relaxed and nurturing. The older two had schooled us in the do's and don'ts of parenting, and over the years we had studied and conducted parenting classes for younger parents at church.

"Africa taught me that children enrich your world like nothing else can," Pat says. "Nathan, before you were even conceived, I would imagine you in your car seat next to me."

Nathan looks over at his mom with a smile and sets his glass of water down.

I'll never forget Pat telling me, "Mark, you need another son." After my initial shock, I said, "Why not two?" Those were happy days. Our mission had made great progress. The Bible School grew from fifty-three students to 243, and the church we started was 1,000 strong. I had just gotten my doctorate and published my first book. Life was on the up and up.

"Nathan, after you were born," Pat says, "we decided to try for one more till I turned forty. I said to the Lord, 'If you give me another baby, you can use that child any way you want.' Five years passed and right before my fortieth, I got pregnant."

"I remember asking you, as adamantly as I could, 'When am I getting my little brother?' Nathan says. "You thought you'd have another little girl. But I asked God for a little brother."

"At eight months," Pat says, as she squeezes a lemon slice into her water, "I had a scan. 'Your baby is hydrocephalic,' the technician said. 'The image shows water around the brain.'"

"What does that mean?" Elesha asks.

"The baby's head is enlarged, and it happens to babies when their moms are older. It is one of the most common brain disorders. It causes a lot of long-term developmental problems."

At that point, we knew we were having a boy and had chosen the name Ethan, a Bible character renowned for his wisdom and mentioned in comparison to Solomon.

"The next evening," Pat says, "we were at a church. The pastor's wife, said, 'Your child will help bring his generation to God.' She prayed for Ethan, and the following day I went into labor. His birth was glorious. The midwife cradled him in her arms. He wasn't hydrocephalic at all. 'Well, hello, Ethan!' she said, and wrapped him in a warm blanket. He was a gift to us."

Gently touching Pat's arm, Elesha says, "I went to the hospital to meet Ethan. You held him with great pride as we all sat in that huge hospital bed around him."

Looking down at his glass of water, Johnathan says, "Strange that a scan showed a dark spot on Ethan's head."

Ethan's life ended with a blow to his head as if that scan picked it up all those years ago before he tasted the goodness of life. Makes me think of Psalm 139:16: "Your eyes saw my substance, being yet unformed. And in your book they all were written, the days fashioned for me, When as yet there were none of them."

Our food arrives, and plates and bowls are passed around the table.

"When Ethan was a few months old," Pat goes on to say, "we visited America. He went everywhere with me. He sat alert in the stroller while I shopped and met people. He didn't catnap the whole day. He was different from you guys in that way. Grandma picked up on it. After babysitting him, she said, 'There is something wrong with your baby. He doesn't sleep at all.' It was as though Ethan was determined to get as much out of each day as possible."

"Mom, you're right," Elesha says. "Ethan's energy level was always off the charts."

His load of classes, his homework, his training with the team during the week, his weekend jobs—showing homes and refereeing kids' soccer—his evening at Young Life, and his doing street ministry, all made him one busy boy. And then to volunteer his Saturday to measure the hammer throws. It was too much for anyone.

"Judy was a big help to us," Pat says, as a lifetime of memories beckons to be heard amidst the clamor of our forks and knives.

Judy was always cheerful, and she helped us raise Ethan. When he would fuss, she would insist, "That's not your way." From the time he was a toddler, she also taught him to share what he had. Years later, when I planned a visit to Zimbabwe, Ethan, age fourteen, insisted, "Give this to Judy," and he handed me five $20 bills, all the money he had. Because of Judy, the sweetness of the Shona people lived in Ethan's heart. He took to Africa like a native plant. Africa was like a mother to him.

"You remember what Ethan said when we visited America and he saw his first snowfall?" Johnathan asks.

In a few brief hours, twenty-one inches of snow had blanketed Cincinnati. Once plowed, the snow rose in tall, unbroken piles on either side of the street, like a long white tunnel. As I drove, Ethan, who was five at the time, sat in the back, leaning casually on the middle armrest as he commented on our winter wonderland.

"'It's the work of God!' he said," and Johnathan gives us all a big smile.

"Most Cincinnatians would've questioned his assessment," I add with a grin, imagining them sliding in their cars, slipping on the snowy pavement, and cursing the elements as they trekked about.

"Something I remember from that trip," Nathan says. "We were driving somewhere, and you were listening to a radio preacher. The guy spoke in a slow monotone, and Ethan said, 'And blah, blah, blah!'"

Johnathan and Elesha laugh.

"Yeah," I add, "he was parroting his older siblings' latest idiom."

"I remember," Johnathan says, "driving to that church in Over the Rhine, and Ethan said, 'Looks like a place where gangsters would hide out.'"

Ethan, ever observant, had us chuckling again.

Working with the homeless at the Respite Center in Cincinnati for five years, Johnathan got to know that notoriously rough neighborhood.

"Whenever I'd come home," Johnathan says, "Ethan would demand a big hug and a kiss on the forehead. He'd have a mischievous smile that said, 'I'm glad you are home. Let's play.'"

"When he was about seven," Johnathan continues, "I heard banging noises coming from his bedroom. I opened the door and found him playing Fifa. 'They scored in the last second. The ref denied a penalty for my team!' Ethan protested. His face was red as he paced back and forth, glaring at the TV monitor in disbelief. You remember our old Panasonic video. Well, I videoed him, acting like a reporter who was interviewing him. He was amused by my interest and described the match in vivid detail. And then he started laughing hard at what had happened."

Johnathan shakes his head, grabbing his sandwich.

"I remember taking Ethan shopping each year he was in high school," Elesha pipes up. "You know, he never asked much for things. So, each summer's end, I'd ask him. 'What's on your list?' I never told him how much we could spend, and when I reached the amount that I'd set aside, I'd pull out another shirt or wild pair of socks, but Ethan would stop and say, 'No, no, this is enough!' His unselfish attitude made me want to give to him even more."

Like every teenager, Ethan would've loved to have the latest video game, but growing up in Zimbabwe, he saw what it really meant to go without, and he accepted that there were things he wasn't going to have. Also, he didn't want to put financial pressure on me.

"I got some messages earlier," Nathan says, picking up his phone.

"Could you read them to us?" Pat asks.

"From Brendon," Nathan says. "'Dear Ethan, I'll always remember our times in Zimbabwe when we ran wild in the yard, picking buckets of mulberries and leaving with stains all over our hands and faces. We swam in the pool with a backpack on as if we were Navy Seals, and we got in trouble for melting army men and sticking them to the wall. You will always be my childhood best friend.'"

"From Takudzwa: 'At Heritage School, Ethan was my first friend. Whenever I was with him, he brought out my inner joy; even up to now I'm grateful for ever meeting him. I was made aware of his death five minutes before reaching out to you.'"

"The news has reached Zimbabwe," Johnathan says.

The mood suddenly feels somber again. I look over at Elesha, then at Pat, and Pat stretches out her hand and looks at her wedding ring as if it's a wristwatch.

"Our first year back from Africa, I lost one of the four diamonds in my ring. Each one represented one of you. When I lost it, I thought, 'Oh God, I would never want to lose a child.'"

After we had spent twenty years together, Pat designed a wedding ring in place of the gold band I gave her on our wedding day. I remember when she lost one of the diamonds.

"Before Ethan died," Elesha says, "I had a weird feeling. I can't explain it, but when I came to the house, I kept worrying he was never coming home again. Here is my last text to him," Elesha continues. "'Hi, Chugie, you've been on my mind lately. I just wanted you to know how proud I am of you! I'm praying for you! Let me know if there is anything you need. I love you very much!' Here is Ethan's response: 'Thanks Elesha!!! Thanks for the prayers. I'm doing well, just very, very busy and lots happening all the time. I love you lots and lots.'"

I bring up a text from Ethan on my phone and say, "When I told him that Michael Huggins had died of a heart attack. Ethan said, 'We'll see Michael again soon!' That was just before his winter recess. You know he and Michael talked a lot at church. Here is what I said to him. 'What a day that will be when we see Michael again. You've got one week of school, and I get to see you again. Come and see me.' I never would've thought that Ethan would see Michael before me."

"Here's a picture of Ethan on Instagram," Nathan says, as he passes his phone around.

Ethan is smiling and wearing a purple shirt. His roommate, Kyle, posted it: "Ethan, you showed me nothing but kindness." In the picture, Kyle and another volunteer are standing in front of Ethan, holding a rusty steel ball. It must have been taken minutes before he died.

The waitress brings the bill, and she sets it on the placemat in the empty space to my left.

"You see that empty chair?" I say to my family, pointing to the chair next to me. "When we sat, my first instinct was, 'Get up and move it away from your table.' But you remember those strange thoughts, which floated through my mind as I woke? 'Do I have three or four children?' Well, our table has six seats because I have four children. We're a family of six, and that empty chair is there to remind us that one of us is absent."

My heart aches as I say it, and a wave of grief sweeps over me, but I couldn't keep from saying it, and now whenever we gather, Ethan's absence will be as noticeable as our being together, his silence as loud as our speech. And what will we do, if God is silent, and he doesn't tell us why our beloved is continually absent?

·9·

Leaving Africa

(A DECADE PAST)

....

"But the place remains in your heart forever!"

....

TEN YEARS AGO, my biggest question was very different, and I wonder now if Ethan would still be alive if we had decided to stay in Africa. Ethan didn't want to leave Africa. He was nine when I told him we were moving back to America. Tears filled his eyes, and I tried to be upbeat, saying, "We'll be near Johnathan and Elesha!" A tear fell to his checks, and I tried a cliché: "It's the people who make the place!"

"But the place," Ethan said, "remains in your heart forever!"

Never were truer words spoken, and as if transported back in time, I see myself in our Harare home, packing family pictures. I'm all alone. My family is already in America, the younger boys at a new school, and Johnathan and Elesha at college, soon to graduate. It was November 2007.

After our many years in Zimbabwe, we were returning to start a new life in Cincinnati, to enjoy all the opportunities America afforded. I distinctly recall thanking God that we had not experienced the loss of life or limb during our many years in Africa. I thought, *We're returning to the safety and security of the United States.* It was that kind of thought you remember; you know as if you had said it out loud, or as if it flashed before me in neon light, and I thanked God for his protection during our many years in Africa.

Standing in our hallway, I took our pictures off the wall and wrapped them in newspaper before gently boxing them. Each picture was full of memories: our children growing taller, our family growing from two to four children, pictures of health, faces filling out and bodies robust. God had kept us from diseases such as malaria, cholera, TB, and a host of other maladies. He had kept us safe from the wild, rough edges of Africa.

We were on Lake Kariba. The place teems with wild game. Hippos, their big eyes and round noses, bob up above water level, accompanied by their attention-getting behavior as they release a loud breath of sprayed water into the air, and again they're out of sight. Close to the shoreline, elephants can't be hidden as they scratch their butts on trees. In the distance, others gracefully reach for leafy branches on tiptoe, like comic ballerinas. A friend from Michigan took my boys on the lake to view a herd on the water's edge. But the motor on his boat stalled, and he drifted toward the large mammals. A mother of a calf angrily flapped her ears and did two mock charges while I rushed in another boat with a rope to pull them out of danger, and again, God kept us from harm.

That evening, we watched the sun go down, setting the lake on fire in yellow hues of light until the waters, as far as the eye could see, quenched the fiery ball. Then, darkness came, and the reflection on the water of an exceptionally bright full moon created an atmosphere of being in another world. We retired, peacefully falling asleep in a houseboat near Spurwing Island.

Beauty and danger, grace and hardness, spirit and flesh, society and wildness live side by side in Africa. But we suffered no harm.

A visit to Manna Pools epitomized our years in Africa. During the height of the political unrest during Robert Mugabe's rule, Steve Griebling visited us. A psychologist, Steve had done crisis counseling at Ground Zero after 9/11. For us, he taught 200 church leaders how to care for the hurting, preached six church services, did lessons at a Bible college, spoke to pastors on "Leading in Times of Extraordinary Stress," addressed two school assemblies, and held a Family Life evening for parents about raising well-adjusted children.

Steve deserved a break, and we set off for a remote game camp on the Zambezi River. The third set of dirt roads was slow and bumpy, and we hadn't seen a soul for hours, but what concerned me were the many tributaries to the Zambezi. Although it was the dry season and the riverbeds were filled with sand, we barely made it across the last one. Abruptly, the wooded terrain ended. I slammed on the brakes. Before us lay a riverbed five times the width of anything we'd crossed. Perched atop the embankment, I looked at the sand and small pools of water dotted on the riverbed, and then I looked across the car seat at Pat and Steve. What choice did we have?

Down the bank, engine revving, tires spinning, the vehicle slid sideways, and we lost traction. We were bogged down in the sand, a quarter of the way across in lion territory. Steve and I slowly got out, and just as we realized that our situation was desperate, a Land Rover appeared at the top of the far bank. Down it flew, confidently coming to a stop alongside us. It had a mechanical winch mounted on its front. A black man and a white man popped out, said hello, and went to work. They towed our car across the sand and up the other bank in fifteen minutes. Then they waved goodbye and were gone.

That's how it was for us in Zimbabwe. It was as if God had assigned two big angels to look after us all our days in Africa, as if he were somehow personally obliged to protect us. He shielded us day and night. How many times God intervened in Africa only he knows. But wherever we went, we were protected and had favor with all the people we met. My confidence in God's ability to keep us safe grew large over the years.

But now this happens in the land of safety!

As if it were yesterday, I still see myself packing our pictures as nightfall came, locking the gates and shutting the windows to our house in Harare. We had three attempted burglaries, during the witching hours, when thieves climbed the wall and poked a hole in a window. But they never got inside. When they lifted the handle to open the window and climb in, the alarm blared, warning us of potential intruders, and off they ran without our TV or video player.

Many nights, however, we had no electricity and no way to know if intruders had breached a door or a window and were now inside . . . and there was no 911, and the police had no vehicles to come to our house, and I had no gun. I'd decided I'd rather trust God than shoot someone. For God does not slumber or sleep. Yet, hooded men robbed our Christian friends, and in an unimaginable horror, a couple that came to our church watched as their teenaged son was shot in the head and killed. The boy had surprised thieves who were confronting his mom.

But God kept us from violent criminals, invisible diseases, accidents on the road, dangerous animals in the wild, and racial rhetoric from self-serving politicians—and now I can't help wondering how things would be with Ethan if we had stayed in Africa.

God always intervened in Africa! He never allowed us to be harmed.

Our African home was a refuge, a place of love and rest, a place I will always cherish. Saying goodbye to her was hard. She was always there for us. She had a peaceful spirit and a clean and orderly character. When we came through her doors after a day's work, she put her welcoming arms around us. She never failed to offer us food at her table, showers in her waters, and a night's rest in her beds. She was God's gift to us. But I stripped her walls of our pictures, emptied her shelves of our goods, and laid bare her floors. Yet never once did she allow the turmoil outside our gates to harm us during our long sojourn in Africa.

Ethan loved his home in Africa. It was a place of play, of childhood memories.

"Hall Ball, me and you invented it," Ethan exclaimed.

Our long hall at home had Elesha's bedroom door on one end and Mom's and Dad's on the other. We kicked a small orange rubber ball back and forth and off the walls to get it into the defender's bedroom for a goal. The ball had short spikes like a porcupine and would bounce at odd angles. It was great fun, and Ethan, age six, didn't like to lose.

We also created a long soccer pitch in our backyard with goals on each end. There we often played in the late afternoon before our family had dinner around the table. Ethan loved playing soccer in his yard. With two acres surrounded by walls on three sides and a fence in the back, it was his first world. Only once did he feel threatened there. He was seven years old when a baboon with big ugly teeth came onto our property. At age ten when we were in America, he described that day for his classmates in a school paper he titled "The Baboon."

"It's a baboon," Nathan said, as if he were asking a question. We ran inside the house and looked out the small kitchen windows to see what was going on. "What about Shadow?" I blurted out! As soon as I got the words out, you could see our dog wandering closer and closer to the random baboon. I ran into the living room closer to him and opened the window and screamed "Come here, Shadow!" A normal dog would come over and lick you, but Shadow is different. We sent him to Obedience School, and he just came back and does the opposite of what you tell him. So, he just turned and stared at me.

Then my brother came over with crackers. So of course, Shadow saw those and came galloping over in a second. He went to town on those little things, and the next thing you know they were gone. Then my mom suddenly appeared with a camera, and when Shadow saw her taking pictures, he ran over, growling at the baboon who was now only a few meters away from the house. "No!" my mom said sternly to Shadow, and he looked away from the baboon and—surprise—he walked back to the window where we were watching this unfold.

Baboon's teeth are big. If Shadow got in a fight with him, we wouldn't have a dog anymore. My dad, who was totally oblivious to all of this, came over. "What are you all looking at?" That scared the death out of me. "There's a baboon in the garden," Nathan said in disbelief. "Madam, be careful!" Umbuya Judy shouted out the window to my mom. "I know she could die," Nathan said. As soon as I heard that I just started to cry furiously. "Aacckk, Ethan, don't waste your water! Mommy's all right," Umbuya said. "Don't waste your water," is her most famous saying that she would say when I would cry. The baboon just stared at us from his perch on top of one of our trees, as if he owned the place. Then after a few minutes, he got less interested and hopped over the wall and was gone.

The baboon scared Ethan, but for me the creature was no threat to us. Later, it was fun to talk about. It was as if the baboon had come to simply amuse us, and as I packed our belongings, I thanked God that the dangers in Africa were never allowed to harm us. And it was then that I thought to myself, we're moving to America, and I don't need to worry about our safety anymore.

Ethan was right. The place was good to us. Better than I had anticipated. Africa gave us more than we gave her. We went to Africa with two children and returned with four, and our children grew up in her rain-soaked soil like well-watered plants around our table. She was our safe haven. Often, I dream of her, and even while awake, memories of her kindness call out to me above the rumbling of Nathan's car and my exhausted body.

Ethan loved our black Labrador, Shadow. We had two black Labs in Zimbabwe. Clare, the first one, died when Ethan was two and a half. The week after Clare died, four mornings in a row, Ethan asked me, "Where's Clare?" We had to get another.

Ethan and I talked about Shadow after we relocated to America. We had to leave him behind. He always ran to greet us when we got home, and we imagined him running to the gate each time a car came, hoping it was us. Tears filled Ethan's eyes and he got quiet. "He lives on a farm now," I told him. "He's happier. He has more space to run around." Ethan asked, "Are you sure he's still alive?" I told him, "Oh, yes! He had three to five years left in dog lifetime."

But where did Ethan's fifty to sixty more years on earth go?

My heart was full when we left Africa, and now grief hemorrhages out of me, too much heartache bottled up inside, though my memories take me back to better days.

"Dad," Johnathan says, tapping me on the arm, "Were you sleeping?"

I wish I was. Wish I hadn't left Africa. Wish I wasn't here. Wish Ethan could live a normal lifespan.

"Dad, you need to read this article before we talk to the police."

I see the headline: "Safeguards under scrutiny after student dies in Wheaton hammer throw."

Wheaton police said Monday they're trying to unravel a mystery in the death of Wheaton College student Ethan Roser: How was he struck by a hammer throw when he was standing in an area that should have been safe? Deputy Chief Bill Murphy said "the throw that struck

Roser appeared to be off-angle, and that the freshman transfer student was outside the lines marking the area where the hammer was supposed to land. Things like this are not supposed to happen," he said. "What broke down at this point, I don't know." NCAA rules require that hammer throw competitions use a safety cage that partially surrounds the thrower and is meant to keep the weight from traveling off course. Wheaton College has one standing in a corner of Lawson Field, where the event took place. Wheaton College did not respond to questions about precautions it had in place for the event. Hammer throwers generate momentum by spinning before releasing the weight, and if they let go too soon, it's supposed to crash into the cage's netting and fall harmlessly to the ground. Larry Judge, a former track and field coach at the University of Florida and now a kinesiology professor at Ball State University, has written about safety issues within hammer throwing. He said the NCAA's requirements for safety cages fall short of those enacted by the International Association of Athletics Federations. Cages for international competitions must be 6 and 1/2 feet taller than those required by the NCAA and have "doors"—panels that can be shifted to adjust the opening for right- and left-handed throwers—about six inches wider. The larger dimensions narrow the "danger zone" where the hammer can travel, Judge said.

(*The Chicago Tribune*, Joe Mahr and Phil Rosenthal, April 24, 2017)

·10·

An Ongoing Investigation

....

*"Now that school just means learning a bunch of
crazy stuff about God and the Bible,
I am not really sure how I made it through high school."*

....

WE ARRIVE AT THE WHEATON POLICE STATION on West Liberty Drive. Outside, three concrete columns rise from the pavement to support two long lintels. Fifteen feet overhead, they create a right angle that leads us to glass entrance doors. Meeting the police here makes more sense than meeting with them at the college, but what do they do in a case like this?

Inside, windows fill the upper half of an interior wall, framing a passageway through which we enter a room and sit at a long conference table. Detective Uhlir positions himself at the head of the table and opens a file. Another detective sits in the corner. Both detectives are clean cut and dressed in smart-casual attire.

"In my twenty years with the department," Uhlir says, "we've never had so many calls on a case as we've had for Ethan. I believe that's a tribute to the type of person your son was."

"Thank you," my family and I utter.

"When I got to Lawson Field, they were still performing CPR on him."

The officer sitting in the corner frowns and shakes his head, sympathetically.

"It happened during warm up. Three to four throws were made in rapid succession. It was an errant throw by an Aurora student. It traveled 138 feet in the air. The volunteers were told not to turn their backs to the cage."

My hands tighten their grip on the armrests of the chair. Why is he repeating that narrative? I can't just listen this time and accept that Ethan was the cause of the accident.

"We just came from the coroner. He said the hammer hit Ethan on the side of his head."

Uhlir looks down at his file and says, "A volunteer who had just returned a hammer said he saw Ethan turn at the last second. He must've turned when people shouted, 'Watch out!'"

"We were told that the hammer that killed Ethan barely missed hitting that boy by a couple of feet. He had just returned a hammer, and then he heard that one whiz over his head. If Ethan was further away from the cage than he was, and he saw Ethan turn, he must have also had his back turned, since that hammer traveled around sixty miles an hour."

Uhlir looks at the detective sitting in the corner but doesn't say anything.

Lord, help me to keep my cool. It will not help if I get angry. But I don't get it.

"Did the boy," I ask, lowering my voice, "whom the hammer grazed after it hit Ethan see anything?"

I catch myself before I add, *And did that boy also have his back turned?*

"We just found out it hit another young man," Uhlir says. "He was not there when I arrived. This morning I was informed that he was taken away to see if he needed medical care."

Good! He's honest about not knowing until today that another boy was hit by the same hammer that killed our son.

"We were at Lawson Field yesterday," I say. "School officials tried to explain what happened. But honestly, we still don't understand how it happened."

"I'm sure Wheaton College will cooperate fully," Uhlir says. "Our job is really to see if there was intent by anyone in a criminal manner to hurt your son."

"We feel sorry for the boy who threw the hammer," I say. "We would never blame him. There has got to be more to it than him not looking before he threw the hammer or the boys having their backs turned. They're all victims."

While I wait for Uhlir to reply, he looks around the table at my family, and then he says, "Our investigation is ongoing, and it will not be complete until we hear back from the coroner. He must first do lab work to see if there were any drugs or alcohol in Ethan's body."

You're not going to find—I want to say it but don't—any of that stuff in his body. *The police are just doing what they do.* But why only scrutinize the one who dies who can't say anything to defend himself?

"When our report is ready, you can download it online," Uhlir says.

"Sir, we appreciate what you're doing," Johnathan says.

Since it's not a criminal case, they'll not do anything more than file a report, and our conversation has gone about as far as it can go.

"Thank you, Officer," I add, and we all get up, and I shake hands with both detectives.

But I can't accept that the cause of Ethan's death is that he had his back turned.

Once we're out the door, I ask Nathan, "Please phone the president's office at Wheaton. Let Ryken know we want to meet with him again. We'll wait as long as it takes to see him."

Just an hour later, we're at the Harbor House on Wheaton's campus, sitting in a well-appointed lounge. Johnathan and Pat share a sofa, as do Elesha and Nathan. Phillip Ryken fills an upholstered chair to my right, and across from me, Paul Chelsen sits on a comfortable wing-back. A polished wooden coffee table is situated between us.

Best for me to begin with small talk.

"Do you have children?" I ask Ryken, leaning back in my chair.

"Yes, I have five."

"Wow, that's a quiver full!"

Ryken rests his hands on the armchair and says, "Our community will always remember your words to our students at chapel last night."

"We felt lots of compassion from everyone," I reply, looking at Pat for agreement.

Ryken nods and listens for more.

"We heard that the young man from Aurora who threw the hammer was so distraught that he went straight home and doesn't plan to finish the semester."

"We don't want him to carry any guilt," Johnathan says, continuing my thought. "We'd like to assure him of that. Maybe we could write him a note?"

"That's not necessary," Ryken says. "I will certainly communicate that to his school."

Ryken then looks at me with a questioning glance as to the purpose of our meeting.

"Okay, well, we have three points we want to discuss with you."

Looking down at my notes, I see my sister's text message suggestion.

"We'd like to set up a scholarship fund for ministry students as part of Ethan's legacy. When Ethan looked at transferring to Wheaton, costs were a big concern. I'm sure that's a concern for most students."

"Well, we do have several scholarships in memory of people. We fund them from investments, starting with a minimum of $25,000. You could write a tribute to Ethan, something we would give scholarship recipients."

"That would be first prize, to do a scholarship with Wheaton. But we have a big concern about Ethan's legacy, and others remembering him for who he truly was." I learn forward in my chair. *How can I best say this to him?* "Our son was involved in supervised activities his whole life. He followed instructions. He can't speak for himself now, and we don't want him blamed. Something else went wrong . . ."

"Something definitely went wrong," Chelsen exclaims. "Someone died! We met this morning with all our staff that was part of the event to discuss that."

That someone was my son—*Don't say that, Mark*—he means "someone" in a rightful sense.

"Is there a rule book or something you follow for these events?" I ask.

"The NCAA has a handbook that provides rules and guidelines," Chelsen says. "The athletic department felt it was their best set up ever for the event."

"We'd never want another family to have to go through this!" I reply. *If that was your best setup then how did my son die?*

"I've instructed the athletic department to review all our throwing competitions," Ryken says, shoulders rising in his chair. "There'll be none held on our campus until that is complete."

"We believe God has a reason for allowing our son's death, but I need to tell you this: It doesn't negate your responsibilities. Jesus' death was planned by God, and yet he held Judas, Pilate, and the Sanhedrin responsible for the roles they played in his death. Not that I equate

Wheaton with their evil actions, but the principle of responsibility remains true, and I need to know what happened!"

"We're cooperating with the police in every way possible," Ryken says. "We'll be transparent, I assure you. We can't expect God to bless the school unless we conduct ourselves in a Christian manner."

The word "bless" strikes me as odd, and I take a deep breath as I decide to ask him up front.

"As a pastor, I was always required to have insurance for venues and events. What insurance does the school have for accidental deaths during supervised activities?"

Ryken looks at his vice president and says, "Paul will have to get back to you on that."

Chelsen writes something on a notepad.

"Okay," I say. "We've had a long day."

"We are praying for you," Chelsen says. His boss nods in agreement, and we all get up.

I'm worn out, and my family looks exhausted too.

While walking to our cars, Nathan says to me, "You handled that really well."

"I don't know. I had a lot more I wanted to say!"

"Dad, I would've probably gotten angry and said things I would later regret."

I've never dealt with anything like this. Nothing even close. It's happened so fast. None of it makes any sense!

· 11 ·

Possible Answers

....

"We take things that help us understand God better,
but over time we make them into idols.
Reality is such that God will kick out the walls of
our human temples, so he can reveal more of himself to us."

....

THE NEXT DAY, we arrive back in Cincinnati as night falls. The tree lines fade and the woods outside our house seem unfamiliar. The family will all stay at our house until Ethan's memorial service—their presence with us is a welcome respite.

Stacked on the floor all over the living room are copies of our book, *My African Dream*. The memoir of our years in Zimbabwe had arrived at our house the day before Ethan died. The timing of its publication feels strangely fated. In the last chapter, I wrote: "Ethan, our youngest, is now on the launch pad, fuel burning rapidly as he fills up on the Bible at Wheaton College and is rocketed God knows where."

"Rocketed God knows where"—*I would've never thought . . .*

After dinner, I asked the family to help me prepare a mail-out of our book. We prepare 200-some copies, then Pat, Holly, Perry, and Elesha go off to bed. It's midnight, and Nathan is sprawled out on our sofa with his feet up, placing letters in books, and Johnathan is stretched on the chaise lounge, stuffing books in envelopes. Sitting in a wingback chair, I peel off address labels, stick them on the front of the envelopes as we attempt to finish the job. Nathan gets up and hands me a letter from his stack.

"You don't need an envelope for this one," he says, "but you might want to keep it."

I sigh as I read my letter to Ethan: "Your mom and I could not be more pleased than we are with you. This is our story, an account of the life we've shared." Two weeks ago, on our mission stationery, I wrote a personal letter to each of our partners. I also wrote a letter to each of our children to place in a copy of our book for them.

Nathan steps over books on his way to the kitchen and I hear him open the fridge.

Looking over at Johnathan, I say, "You know how when you open too many programs on your computer, that rainbow circle goes round and round? Well, my brain has circled the 'Why' question for a whole week now."

"Dad," Johnathan says, looking up from the book he's handling, "my first thought after you told me was that God is sparing Ethan from trouble."

Johnathan refers to Isaiah: "The devout are taken away, and no one understands that the righteous are taken away to be spared from evil. Those who walk uprightly enter into peace; they find rest as they lie in death." Abijah is an example. He died in boyhood to escape troublesome days, because "the God of Israel found some good thing in him" (Isaiah 57:1–2, NIV; see 1 Kings 14:13).

"But Ethan was so trouble free. The normal troubles we have in this world? Trouble with women?"

His junior year of high school, Ethan was upset. "What's wrong?" I asked. "I don't want to talk about it!" he shouted as he rushed down the basement steps. A few minutes later, he came upstairs. "Sorry, Dad," and he told me what a girl had said to him. "You're too intense!" She didn't want to date him. "I *was* intense," he explained, "because I really liked her. She wasn't like any girl I've ever met."

Ethan was always quick to apologize and learn from his mistakes.

"I don't know about that," Nathan says, looking over at Johnathan and me before plopping onto the sofa with a steaming bowl of chicken and rice. "Ethan was very level-headed and handled things in stride. God has his reasons, and we may never know why this side of heaven."

In front of me, I flip another envelope onto the sturdy table, made of African teak, adding it to Johnathan's pile. The pace of our work is slowing down, but I think we will finish tonight.

"God doesn't have to tell me why," I admit, "but Jesus did answer his followers' questions. He told Paul why he had a thorn in his flesh. He even told John who it was who would betray him."

Waving at the heat rising from his bowl, Nathan says, "Maybe it's a test. God allowed Satan to test Job to prove his character!"

"After Ethan died, I prayed that his death wouldn't get between any of us and God."

"I don't think it happened simply to test you or our family," Johnathan says, shifting his legs and placing a parcel on the floor. "I mean—God's already tested you in lots of ways. Besides, it is Ethan who died. He had his own relationship to God."

"But nothing has tested me like this. So, let's list some possibilities," I suggest. "One: God took Ethan to spare him from trouble. Two: God has reasons we can't fathom, or he doesn't wish to tell us. Three: It's a test to see if we'll still love God. But I recall that Job got an answer. God allowed the devil to test him: Satan instigated his children's deaths. What other reasons can you think of?"

Placing another label on an envelope, I wait to hear other possible reasons my sons will offer as to why their brother died.

"God is bringing Ethan's friends to Jesus through his death, and thousands of people heard of his faith in Christ," Johnathan says.

"Bringing people to Christ is a good reason. That's four. But I can't help thinking, if Ethan lived a full life, he would've led many souls to Christ. 'The harvest is great, but the workers are few.' So, it doesn't make sense for God to remove a productive worker who'd bring many more to Christ."

"Dad," Nathan looks over at me, "in the early church, Steven was a gifted and fruitful worker. His martyrdom didn't make sense, but it brought Paul to Christ, and Paul reached the then known world for Christ."

"Sharing in the sufferings of Christ," Johnathan says, "can make us more Christlike."

"Five: Ethan's death is like Stephen's; it will lead to a Paul-like worker who will lead multitudes to Christ, and," I add for emphasis, "help bring the return of Christ. Sixth reason: conform me to Christ's image. Make me better. Suffering, however, can also make a person bitter."

My theological sons wait for me to say something more.

"You would both agree it might be helpful to know why?"

"Depending on the answer," Nathan says.

"When we were driving back from Chicago yesterday, I wondered where I've missed it. Opening the door to the devil can be a seventh reason why Ethan died," I say.

"The disciples asked who sinned," Johnathan's voice rises, "that a man should be born blind: him or his parents? 'Neither sinned,' Jesus said, 'but it happened so that the glory of God might be displayed in him.'"

"It was a big belief back then," Nathan says, "that all suffering was due to personal sin."

"Sometimes," I say, "it is. Paul told the Corinthians, 'A man's body is destroyed so that his spirit might be saved.' He also said, 'Some have died because they take communion in an unworthy manner. Because they refuse to judge themselves, God judges them so that they're not condemned with the world. He takes them before they lose their salvation. But that was not the case with Ethan. I forgot how you said it, Johnathan, yesterday at Wheaton, but you said something like, 'it doesn't get any better than this on how Ethan was living for Jesus.' It wasn't Ethan's sin, and if it was mine, doesn't the Bible teach that sons will not die for the sins of their fathers?"

"It sounds like what we are doing is a process of elimination," Nathan says. "Like when something doesn't work on your car or computer, you figure out what it can't be."

While my hands peel an address label, my mind goes to work, searching for another answer.

"I recall from studying theodicy—suffering is partly due to the kind of world God created. Even before Adam sinned, natural laws like gravity made physical suffering possible. Man's dominion over the earth required work and made pain, like aching muscles, possible. Pain warns us that our earthly bodies have limitations. We were made with tear ducts too. Theodicy also argues that the world God created is the very best world he could've created for his eternal purposes or else God wouldn't be perfect in all his ways."

But wouldn't it be a better world if Ethan had not died?

"Where does it say that Adam or Eve suffered before they sinned?" Nathan asks.

"Tests and temptations," I reply, "are a form of suffering. The book of Hebrews says, 'Jesus suffered being tempted.' Before they sinned, Adam and Eve in the Garden suffered temptation. Also, Eve would've had some distress in childbearing, even before sin entered the world. Bear in mind God said he would *increase* Eve's labor pains, and Adam's toil to grow crops."

"But the suffering of death," Johnathan says, "had not entered the world until Adam sinned. Right?"

"That's true. No one had died. Sin had not entered the world. I imagine if they had hurt themselves, God would have healed them."

"If we violate natural laws," Johnathan says, "like speeding around a curve or throwing ourselves from a building, we're testing God and he is not obliged to rescue us."

"But how," Nathan asks, "does all that apply to Ethan and the possible reasons why he died?"

"Our dominion on earth requires acting in a responsible way. God didn't invent the hammer throw, and if we're going to play a game to see who can throw metal weights the farthest, we must provide a safe environment."

"We've got another possible reason," I continue. "Ethan's death is simply the result of not being safe. Kind of like testing God by throwing yourself from the pinnacle of the temple."

Johnathan continues to stuff books in envelopes, while Nathan places letters in books.

Then Nathan says, "On the testing God reason, doesn't he decide? I mean God ultimately decides when a person will die, even if they are being stupid like driving too fast. People often do stupid, dangerous things, and God keeps them alive because it isn't their time to die. I think we can eliminate the testing-God reason for Ethan's death."

"Maybe I set myself up for a Job-like test by writing a book on the devil and God's sovereignty?"

"Dad, God knew how you'd respond," Johnathan says, as he stretches his arms behind his head. "He doesn't give us more than we're able to handle. And this isn't just about us. A child of God, named Ethan, died."

Nathan places his empty bowl on an end table with a clang and Johnathan shifts his body.

"Ethan asked me a month ago, 'Dad, what do you believe about predestination?' I told him predestination is based on God's foreknowledge. But just because God knows things in advance, that doesn't mean he causes them. He knew Adam would sin. . . ."

"Oh, Dad, sorry to interrupt you but that reminds me . . ." Johnathan reaches for his phone. "Sammy sent me a text that I've been meaning to show you. Here it is:"

> Nathan, Ray, Johnathan, and I would often debate theological issues. Predestination and that kind of stuff. It always lasted for hours and usually got intense. Ethan didn't say much during our debates. He'd be playing on Xbox. After all of us were done saying what we could and were too stubborn to admit defeat, Ethan would say something. He never chose sides, but what he said cut through it all, something that showed we were caught up in things that ultimately didn't matter in our own day-to-day moments. He did that more than once, and I remember thinking, "Well, I can't argue with that."

Johnathan flips his phone down on the sofa. "Maybe it's a combination of the things we talked about!"

"It could be none of the reasons we came up with," Nathan says. "I don't think it will matter in eternity."

"And God can use it for good," Johnathan adds.

Only God can, and I've thought about how experts invariably advance to the more difficult, leading up to their grand finale. The difficulty factor is true in every field of endeavor: mathematicians solving harder equations; Einstein pondering the nature of light, time, and space. I've never struggled like this with "why?" But I've never been hurt like this before.

"It's okay, Dad," Nathan says, tenderly. "It's going to take time."

"I believe God will show you," Johnathan says, getting up and giving me a hug.

My sons see that their old man has gone quiet. He doesn't have the answer this time.

· 12 ·

My American Nightmare

....

"Kind of spooky out there!"

....

IT'S STILL DARK OUT WHEN I WAKE. Life has lost its sense of rhythm. It's like there are no mornings or evenings, days or nights, springs or summers—only yesterdays and years gone by.

Quietly, I retreat to my office. My desktop screen reads 2:32 a.m.

Outside, the wind blows. A storm is brewing, and I shut my office window. Then, a flash of lightning and a boom of thunder announce that heavy rains are headed our way. Then the house is quiet again.

Ethan's voice plays in my head. "Kind of spooky out there!"

We had moved to this secluded property three years ago, and one night dense fog blanketed our unfinished house. As I got out of my car, it felt spooky, like in a scary movie. Hearing someone in the house, Ethan, age sixteen, met me in the kitchen with those words and a grin on his face.

Ethan had introduced me to "night terrors." On a handful of occasions at night until he was about six years old, he would suddenly bolt upright in bed at night, screaming and thrashing around hysterically, his heart beating fast and his shirt wet with sweat. The episodes lasted a couple of minutes, and he would be inconsolable until he was fully awake. Later, he had no recollection of what had happened.

"I wish you would wake me from the terrors of the past week," I mutter, looking at his picture on my desk.

Grief feels much worse than fear. I could face fear and fight it off or flee from it. But with grief who do I fight? Where do I run? I'm restless and disoriented. Fear has made good its most terrible threat against me. Grief is fear fully realized. My stomach continually flutters. Each passing minute is dreadful; there's no end in sight.

Raindrops appear on my window, increasing in frequency and intensity, while I read the notes that sit on my desk.

Marrilo: "Ethan's death hit me like a bomb. I just covered my face and wept. My son, Marcin, has cried for the first time since childhood."

Bob: "I was working at 'After the Prom' when our students heard about Ethan's death. The outpouring of love from the kids was unbelievable."

Michael: "I was at a party at my girlfriend's house. I was helping people carry food down the basement steps. Ethan's picture flashed on my phone with the headline, 'Wheaton College Freshman Killed.' I collapsed on the steps, crying, screaming, and struggling to breathe. I lay at the bottom of the steps for three hours. My dad had to come to take me home."

Kyle: "When I heard Ethan had died, I never felt such pain and sadness. That evening in Mason, twenty of us met to talk about him. Ethan was the only person who'd ask me, 'How are you doing? Is there anything you want me to pray about?'"

More written responses: "We could not stop crying when we heard the news . . ." "My husband does not cry easily . . ." "It has been years since I cried . . ." "We have no words, only tears . . ."

Tears stream down my face, tears answering tears. Ethan's death has created a great outcry, a throng of hearts, full of pain, amplifying the question—why?

My son, I must make you live again. Make your amazing eyes speak again!

I take a long look at Ethan's picture on my desk. His eyes are radiant and playful. It's as if perpetual laughter resided in those eyes, a delight with life and a love for everything around him. It was as if he knew a great secret about life that few had discovered, and if you could only see life through those eyes, you, too, would know the Mystery.

For a week now, Isaiah's question has pierced my heart: "Who shall declare his generation? for he was cut off out of the land of the living" (53:8).

I rub my weary eyes as memories appear like apparitions, memories of Ethan as an infant and a toddler, memories of bedtime, reading *My Little Golden Book About God* to him: "God gives us dreams and plans for our grown-up years. He gives us memories of yesterdays, so that happy times and people we love we can keep with us always in our hearts. For God is love!"[1]

But now, no more dreaming, no plans for his grown-up years, and no more happy times; only a loss of love and memories of yesterdays.

"Document Ethan's words," the silence suggests, "because his words reveal his heart."

"Ethan's Writings," I title a document. He often worked on my desktop PC, and I do a search of his school papers.

Men in Red: I had waited thirteen years for this moment. "Here it comes," whispered my older brother before it boomed out of the stadium speakers. "You'll Never Walk Alone." I felt warm and cold at the same time; pure joy overwhelmed my body and the words to the song trickled out of my mouth along with thousands of Liverpool fans. Tears welled up in my eyes. All I felt was love. How powerful love truly is; it can bring 42,000 complete strangers together to support a cause. And I felt

like a small child again, like I didn't have a worry in the
world. Even as I sit here on my bed looking at the ticket
from that game, I can feel all the emotions as if I were
reliving them. Long ago but so short a time, I was there
living in dream land.

The American Way of Life: At times life can seem
so short. We find ourselves always on the go, always
working, never a spare moment. We go fast because we
can. We think success is measured by the number of our
possessions and not by who we are or what we do. No
wonder the unhappiness. Is it because we forget what
truly matters?

Growing up in the church, I've always heard that just
because you're a child doesn't mean you don't have a role
to play in God's plan. It's easy to hear this statement as
a teenager and understand what people are saying, but
then we can just continue with life as normal. But it hit
me hard when I got home from camp and read again the
Great Commission Jesus issued. Then, I thought about my
senior year of high school, and I saw it as a commission
to go and make disciples of the nation called Mason High
School.

The Church at Ephesus: Paul calls them to imitate God
like a child mimics his father. In Greco-Roman culture,
the family unit was of supreme importance. A child bears
his father's name, and his actions represent what his
family stands for. In the same way, we as children of God
bear his name, and our actions bear witness to the work
Christ has done in our lives.

Ethan's picture on my desk smiles at me as if he approves of my feeble
effort to collect his writings and somehow record his life.

Good idea—I open a file and name it "Ethan's Friends." Our words and actions affect others and they help reveal who we are.

> Chad: "At Mason Middle School, I was a shy and awkward kid, afraid to speak to anyone who I didn't know. While I sat alone with my thoughts, Ethan was consistently the one who would come to talk. Because of his kindness, I've been able to step out of my shell. Many times, even my worst days would end with a smile, because Ethan had talked to me. His devotion to accept others, and his charismatic radiance energized everyone with whom he came in contact."

> Colleen, a Young Life leader: "I went to the Frontier Ranch Camp. We got stranded there and had to sleep on the floor. Ethan humbly chose a spot without any carpet, so others would have the carpeted area. It was an amazing thing for me to watch. I'll never forget it."

> Lisa: "Ethan, a man who danced in the rain and lived life to the fullest."

> Josh: "Ethan's overflowing joy is one of the reasons I started my relationship with God."

> Shari and Tom: "Ethan introduced our son, Dylan, to Young Life."

> Ed: "We will never forget the impact Ethan had on our son's spiritual journey."

Reading their kind words stirs within me a mixture of comfort and pain—comfort in knowing they loved Ethan, but also pain, because such a one was mine and now he is gone.

Isabel: "My freshman year, all the girls would look at Ethan and say he was the type of guy we wanted to marry. You knew that he had a good soul."

Ethan will never fall in love and marry. I'll never get to see whom he would have chosen. I will never hold his children. The one who carries my name died without a descendant.

An electronic version of yesterday's interview with my family appears online, and I open a file and call it "News Reports."

Keith Biery Golick with the Cincinnati Enquirer: "I lost count of how many times they thanked me. At one point, I told them to stop. They didn't. They offered me food. When they returned from Illinois, his family invited me into their home. I left in awe. 'There is a greater good,' Mark Roser, Ethan's father, told me. 'That's why we're doing what we're doing. It's the only thing that has gotten me out of bed since it happened.'

"The Rosers have been fearless, even in the wake of unthinkable tragedy. I wish I had a faith like that. I went to church growing up. I read scriptures during Sunday service and participated in Bible study and youth group. Now, I can't remember the last time I've been to church. But I'll never forget the way Mark Roser described receiving the news about his son's death. In a steady voice, he recalled seeing a police cruiser in the driveway. He told me about his conversation with the sheriff's deputy and about pacing through his living room. His voice changed in an instant. 'Oh, God,' he screamed. 'You're not going to take my son, are you?' His face seized up, turning red. He tried to suppress it. He blinked his eyes to stop the tears, and his grief came out through clenched lips in a high-pitched whistle. That was the first time I cried during our interview. After the interview, the family huddled together and posed for a picture. They asked if they should smile. 'Ethan would have wanted us to smile,' his brother said."

An email from Paul Chelsen at Wheaton also waits for me in my inbox.

Dear Mark,

Following up on our conversation on Monday afternoon, we have been in touch with our insurance companies to better understand any policies that might provide benefits to you.

We have learned there are two potential policies that may provide benefits:

- QBE Athletics Insurance Policy provides a $10,000 payment for loss of life.
- NCAA Catastrophic Injury Insurance Program provides a payment of $25,000.

Given that Ethan was serving as an event official who was spotting, rather than a student athlete, we have been cautioned that these claims may be denied. Nevertheless, we intend to pursue these claims vigorously on your behalf with the insurance carriers.

Grace and Peace,
Paul Chelsen, PhD

I check to see if the windows in the living room are closed. Torrential rain gushes down them, and flashes of lightning illuminate the creek behind our house as it fills with water. Before Ethan went off to college, I told him, "When we have a good rain, we'll launch you from our creek in one of George's canoes. You know our creek flows into the Little Miami, and it flows into the Ohio River. It will be cheaper transport than airfare."

He thought that was funny, but now we launch him on a river of tears, and I don't know why. My question, deeply relational, is like that of a child asking a parent, "Why, my Father?" Jesus understood why he had to die, and that helped him embrace the cross, as painful as it was. He sympathizes with my struggle to understand.

On my way to the bedroom, I turn off my office light. Ethan's key chain sits on my desk. When I asked him if he had a front door key, he didn't think he did, but in his dorm room I found he had two. Now I can't bring myself to lock the front door and I can't explain why. I leave it unlocked and crawl into bed, besieged with pain that he will never come through that door again.

After Ethan went off to college, I often texted him at the end of a day with the words "Night, night!" Moments later, Ethan would respond, "Night, night!" Lying in bed, I hear him say his last "Night, night," and my heart cries out to God.

Was there no other way? Aren't all things possible with you? There had to be another way!

And a huge emptiness gnaws at me. Ethan's death seems so senseless and preventable.

Unable to sleep, I get out of bed again and go to my office as if I forgot something.

Sighing, I type "Wrongful death" into the Google search engine.

"A wrongful death is a legal term describing the death of an individual caused by negligence. Four elements: negligence, breach of duty, causation, and damages. Common causes: Automobile accidents and injury during supervised activities."

·13·

Ethan's Home Going

....

"I can't wait to go to heaven. It'll be so amazing!"

....

ON THE CORNER OF WESTERN ROW and Mason-Montgomery Road in Mason, Ohio, sits Hope Church. Green lawns in front roll up to the church. The structure is clad with shades of light red and blue bricks. The roof is adorned with a tall white steeple and a cross at its pinnacle. On the entrance side, glass windows fill the upper half of the building, and a long-roofed and paved walkway leads to the main entrance doors. Arriving early by myself, I park amidst a handful of cars, which dot acres of blacktop parking.

We should have secured a smaller church. Ethan's college friends are out of town. Some are taking semester exams. Plus, it is a Sunday afternoon. They will have little time to travel before Monday morning. I told Pat, "I don't think we need a big venue. Maybe 500 people will come." But I was outvoted. Now standing inside the empty sanctuary, I think I should've insisted we go smaller. We'll never fill up this huge space.

The church's audio-visual tech arrives, and on a large screen in the front, Ethan's baby pictures start to appear. Same eyes full of wonder, even as an infant, and that amazing smile. Quickly, I redirect my eyes to the vaulted ceiling from which hang chandeliers with candle-shaped light bulbs.

Mark, just get yourself through the next couple of hours.

I force myself to greet a few people who arrive. Then, I join my family in a back room to go over the order of service.

Twenty minutes later, my family and I make our way to the sanctuary. In the foyer, I'm startled by a crowd of people standing, and ushers hastily unfolding chairs for them. "The doors to the sanctuary will be kept open," I'm told by an usher, "so those who sit and stand in the foyer can hear." And the blue carpet of the foyer gives way to a darker shade of gray as my family enters the church, walking down the center aisle. Turning to look at us, somber faces crowd the pews, row after row, from the front to the back, to our right and our left.

Never have I felt so shattered, and yet, as if outside myself, like an observer, I watch us walk to the front in slow motion, reaching at last a pew to the right of the platform.

The pianist strikes a note, and the rustling of 1,000 people getting on their feet at the same time grips my heart. To think, every person has come to honor our Ethan. I feel great love for each of them. I wish to weep but mustn't. I look at the program.

A melodious female voice leads us: "Be Thou My Vision . . . May I reach Heaven's joys, O bright Heav'n's Sun." On the screen, the lyrics pull me into the intensity of the moment.

My life has been dedicated to comforting others when they are hurting. People looked to me for answers, but now I'm the one hurting and asking how God could allow such a thing.

A cameraman from a local television station moves to the side of the platform as Marie Huggins walks up the three steps to the podium.

"Four months ago, my husband died, and Ethan wrote me a note. As I read it," she says, "keep in mind this is a nineteen-year-old guy: 'I just want to say I am deeply sorry for your loss. It was an honor to know Michael. It is very rare to find people like you. The way you have treated us Roser children is something I will never forget. I am praying for you. It is very easy to be focused on the sadness and forget the fact that really Michael was being called home. The real loss is how much we'll all miss him for a short time before we spend eternity together. Thank you for the example you two have been to me.'"

We all sing, "Give me Jesus. You can have all this world. Just give me Jesus. When I come to die, when I come to die, oh, when I come to die, give me Jesus."

What else matters, then?

In adjacent pews sit my mom, my siblings, and their children. Their faces are heartrending.

My daughter gracefully walks to the podium. Dressed in all black, she is as lovely as any mourner the world has known. "Ethan," she says, "was the very best of us: strong, brave, hope-filled, and compassionate. He loved deeply and celebrated others. He may have been my little brother, but there was nothing little about him, and I would give anything," Elesha's voice cracks, "to have just one more day with him."

I fight back tears, which lie right beneath my eyelids like subterranean springs pushing to the surface and ready to flow. Opening and closing my eyes rapidly, I manage to contain a torrent of tears, a floodgate of sorrow.

"It's okay to cry," I told my family. "Just say all that you've prepared." I was really talking to myself, and I'm still afraid if I don't control myself, I'll be a basket case, and we'll all leave feeling worse than when we came.

Nathan stands at the podium. "When you grow up as the sons of missionaries, you quickly learn that the Sunday school answer is Jesus, but you don't understand your brokenness and your need to be rescued by God.

"I could tell that the same hole, not as big or intense as mine, was there in Ethan, so I asked God to bring Ethan close to Himself, like he had done with me. And I watched Ethan get excited about Jesus and become the fourth Roser in our family to study theology—and we laughed about how we're all going to be broke. When Ethan died last Saturday, all I could do was cry out to God that he had shown himself to my little brother."

Nathan finishes, and I hurry to the podium. Pulling out my notes, I fix my gaze on my three children in the front. "Thank you, Nathan, Elesha, and Johnathan for going to Chicago with your mom and me. I don't know how we would've gotten through this past week without you.

"God knows what it feels like to have a son struck down in the prime of life. God had one, unique son. Jesus bled and died. He took the full impact, all the weight of my sin. It hit him like that steel weight hit Ethan. It hit him with deadly force at the cross. It crushed him, so it would not crush me. . . . But oh, how I have wrestled with God to keep my son. How hard it is for me to let go of him!"

Putting the microphone back, I return to my seat. Johnathan passes me and brushes up against the huge flower wreath from Wheaton College. My eyes then meet those of the college chaplain, and I glance at the music trio from Wheaton sitting with him. Also, in a row to my right is Coach Jake and, behind him, the school's soccer team in two rows. Across from them rows and rows full of students—a busload—who, in a single day, are making the ten-hour roundtrip from Chicago. They have all come to mourn with us, and I wish to weep.

My mind spaces out. Then, I hear people laughing. Looking up, I see Johnathan is bending slightly to speak into the microphone.

"And if you knew Ethan," he says, "he was a good-looking guy. He definitely got his looks from my mom's side."

More laughter and I sense a release of tension. Looking over at my side of the family, the Rosers also laugh, thinking what Johnathan said is funny.

"When my dad told me that Ethan was dead, I sat there, stunned and shaken," Johnathan says. "I started to weep. It was like having a head-on crash with an unavoidable reality, moving faster than my mind could bear. And just as I felt the full weight of that moment bearing down, I saw something! I saw Ethan's face. He had a huge smile! And the thought occurred to me, 'Ethan's in heaven.' Light was reflecting off Ethan's eyes, sparkling like a kaleidoscope full of colors. His eyes were darting back and forth as if he could not keep up with the scope of the scene before him. I knew he was gazing at God's splendor. I stopped crying and stillness came over me. His face was so happy, happier than if he played soccer for Liverpool. . . ."

Johnathan gathers his notes from the podium, and Pat passes him on the steps.

"You've heard how Ethan was such a good person," Pat says, "but it was Christ in him. That morning, before he passed, I sat on my sofa, reading Psalm 27 and thanking God for how good he had been to me. When I got to verse five, I read, 'the day of trouble.' I didn't want to think about trouble, but it was like trouble was lurking over in the corner of the room." And Pat points with her left hand to the far corner of the hall.

"Later that day, I got the news that Ethan had died. Such trouble and gloom. But there is a truth I want to leave with you today: God did not create the human heart to despair. I saw great troubles in Africa, but when we would worship God, his presence would lift us out of our sorrow. I can't explain it, but God would restore our souls, and we'd know joy again. . . ."

The vocalist appears back on the stage, and we sing, "I will rise! Jesus has overcome. And the grave is overwhelmed. The victory is won. He is risen from the dead. And I will rise when he calls my name. No more sorrow, no more pain. I will rise on eagles' wings. Before my God, fall on my knees. And rise. I will rise."

As we sing, I feel close to Ethan like we've somehow transcended the terrible gulf that death has formed between us. I could sing "I will rise" all day. But the song ends, and it is announced, "You can now visit with the family at the front of the sanctuary."

A line quickly forms, and my heart is as soft as a newborn's skin. Tears, smiles, hugs, handshakes, friends, relatives, students, high school teachers, players, coaches, young and old, a throng of tenderness.

I recognize Tyler. "You traveled all that way from Dallas?" I ask.

"Several of us did. We had to. Ethan was one of the greatest guys I've ever met."

Many others, some I haven't seen in years, come ever so gently, one after another. Eventually the consoling line dissipates, and the sanctuary empties—except for a handful of young people.

"I'm Nate. We were with Ethan at the Young Life camp last summer."

He shakes my hand, and behind him, a dozen young faces nod their heads, their eyes searching my face.

"Wow, thank you for waiting through that line. You waited a long time."

A young lady steps out from the group. "That was easy. We drove all day yesterday from Nebraska through heavy rains."

"I have a tattoo like Ethan's," Nate chimes back as he unbuttons the top of his shirt.

Everyone laughs as he shows me his tattoo. Nate is a big, handsome, Black guy, football player size. The Hebrew letters on his tattoo are three times the size of Ethan's.

In contrast, standing by Nate is a petite blonde.

"Every afternoon at camp," Katy says, "we'd all be outside, and a pits member had to stay in the kitchen to get ahead on the dishes. It meant you didn't get to interact with the campers. We all avoided that but not Ethan. He always volunteered to stay."

Pat taps me on the shoulder. "Let's get their picture over there," and she points to the huge picture of Ethan smiling, placed on a tripod in the front of the church.

Katy wants to tell me something as she looks at Ethan's blown-up portrait, and while her friends move into position for a photo she says, "Ethan told me, 'I can't wait to go to heaven. It'll be so amazing!'"

Last night, I read Ethan's report on the camp at Frontier Ranch: "If we could have as much fun on earth as we had at camp, then it is impossible to imagine how amazing heaven is going to be."

More than once growing up, Ethan asked me what dying and going to heaven would be like. I tried to make it sound beautiful. Now he knows far more about heaven than I could ever articulate.

We say goodbye to Ethan's friends. It's time to pack up.

I place the large picture of Ethan on my back seat. In the front, I put baskets of flowers and a bag full of sympathy cards. Also, on the backseat I place the long wooden easel and the five-foot wreath arrangement. Tomorrow, we will use these again at Ethan's burial.

In the parking lot, I pull alongside Elesha's car. She and Pat are loading the rest of the flowers.

Lowering my window, I say, "I'll see you at the house."

Like a file opening, my mind's MapQuest plots my route home, determining how best to get there, from street to street, all the way until I'm home. As I pull out onto Western Row with a bump, a basket of flowers next to me wobbles. I reach across the seat to steady it, and my thoughts take me back many years ago to that road in Africa, when I reached across with my hand to keep Ethan from falling off the passenger seat.

We should've died together that day!

·14·

Why Now?

"I like the drive. It gives me time to think."

ETHAN WAS CUDDLED UP NEXT TO ME, his head leaning against me and his feet on his brother. He was four and Nathan was ten. Both were sound asleep in the front seat with no seat belts on. I could still kick myself. The back of our van was loaded with stuff, but that was no excuse.

I had said a tearful goodbye to Elesha the evening before in Johannesburg. My girl was out of the nest, off to America. Pat and Johnathan accompanied her—Pat to get her settled in with friends for her senior year of high school, and Johnathan to return to college.

That feeling of separation, the sense that things will never be the same, sweeps over me.

Before that sad drive, we were all at home together. I was so content. I would've stopped the clock forever. Those were the happiest days of my life, sunny days I'll never forget. Days playing in the yard, evenings eating around the dinner table, and nights all sleeping in our beds.

My mind was occupied, and my heart ached. Just half of my family—Ethan, Nathan, and I—were headed home. The boys had to get back to Harare for school, and I drove north at seventy miles an hour.

When we approached a bus, I slowed down. Driving in Africa demanded patience. To pass a vehicle, you had to enter the oncoming traffic lane, as on country roads in America. So, my long drives in Africa always began with a prayer for safety, and God had a special way of encouraging me: a bird or flock of birds would fly over my car. That always reminded me of Costa Deir, a preacher, flapping his arms like a bird and moving around the pulpit like he was flying. He said, "When you see birds, they have a message for you. 'For if God feeds birds, how much more will he care for you? And if a sparrow doesn't fall to the ground without your Heavenly Father knowing, then how much more does God watch over your life!'" I took the bird messages to heart whenever I drove the long expanses of the African bushveld, and our family road trips were always an anticipated change of scenery.

Outside Masvingo, the terrain changes from small trees and shrubs to stupendous earth mounds, sprinkled with robust balancing rocks, floating on top of smaller rocks. The road then winds in a frenzy through the mountains before it straightens again. In the distance, I would see granite-capped hills, and I would gauge the kilometers. Oh, the beauty and largeness of the African terrain inspired me. It opens your eyes to see a world beyond flesh and blood. Zimbabweans are spiritually sensitive; they believe in an unseen world of spirits, a parallel universe and an existence more real and powerful than human ingenuity. Their spirituality also encompasses the whole range of life, for nothing happens by chance. Everything is caused by forces unseen.

Pat could've lost all three of us that day. . . .

The bus I was following slowed down as it approached a slower-moving truck. It was broad daylight, and I could see the whole road ahead of us. It was an easy pass. Night driving, however, was a different story. Some cars have only one weak taillight to show that they're there. Others come barreling toward you with no headlights at all. Once, in the dark of night, I came upon a man lying facedown in the road. He had been hit and killed. Another time, a giraffe stood with one foot on the road and three feet on the grass. He didn't move as I sped past him. Years ago, with the whole family in the car, I approached a bus that was blowing out a cloud of black smoke. The fumes smelled bad, the sun was setting, and I was in a hurry. As we overtook the bus, a passenger threw a packet of red juice out a window, and it splattered on our windshield. Before I could express my anger through the horn, a still voice spoke in my heart: "That could be your family's blood." My anger gave way to a somber awareness of my responsibility for my family's safety. As a result, I stopped driving long distances at night.

That day, with Ethan in the front seat next to me, I cruised behind this bus for several miles in bright sunshine. When the bus approached a slow-moving truck and made no attempt to overtake it, I was sure the driver wanted me to go first because there was a long stretch of straight open road before us. So, I checked again to make sure no cars were coming toward us in the oncoming lane; then I hit the horn twice to let him know I was going to pass.

As I pulled my Toyota Venture alongside the bus to overtake, all of sudden, the bus started to pull out to overtake the truck. Like a madman, I pressed the horn! How could he not know I'm right here alongside of his bus?

As though it were happening now, I feel the impending doom!

In his blind spot, I was only a third of the way past him as he glided into my lane—a lane hardly wide enough for my vehicle. In a nanosecond, instead of jamming on the brakes, I pushed the accelerator to the floor, standing on the pedal, to go as fast as possible. But the bus continued taking over my lane, and I was partly off the road, a tire on the edge of a steep embankment. I watched gravel fly into the air and over the edge, and my heart was racing faster than the car's engine.

My hand then reached over to steady Ethan's body as he bounced about on the front seat.

At that point, time seemed to shift into slow motion. Off the road we would go, pushed by that bus down the cliff, flipping over and over. I was certain of it.

As the bus took over my lane, I gained just enough speed to somehow squeeze right in front of him, less than a foot between us. I bellowed a loud sigh of relief that woke Ethan and Nathan, and I saw the bus driver's shocked eyes in my rearview mirror, big as life.

Five miles later, I stopped at a gas station, still dumbfounded that he hadn't plowed me off the hillside. The bus driver pulled in behind me. Immediately, he came over, shaking his head, and saying, "Sorry, sorry! I didn't see you. I swear!"

"Did you hear my horn blasting?!?" I demanded.

"The music was up so loud. I thought your hooting was part of the song."

My God, it would've been our death dirge!

Countless times I've rehearsed our dreadful eighty-mile-an-hour dance, repeating each step and its sequence. If I had gone to overtake a second later or slowed down instead of speeding up, or if he had come sooner or more quickly into my lane, we would have been off the road, plunging down the ravine, goners. There was no margin of error in speed or timing. A stunt team couldn't have enacted it as closely and dramatically as it had transpired. And if, somehow, I had survived, I don't know how I would've forgiven myself. The boys would've been thrown from the van and killed, for I alone had a seatbelt on. Ethan was so young. I should've protected him.

And what would Pat have done, if the news she received in Cincinnati had been true?

Our brush with death that day loitered as if the spirit world demanded a hearing. For when I reached Harare, I got an email from Pat. She had tried to use my Visa card in Cincinnati, and it was denied. When she phoned the bank, they told her it was blocked because a notation indicated that "Mark" was dead. Her email went on to explain that the bank had confused me, Mark Clarence Roser, with my dad, Clarence Roser. My dad had managed our account, and I only used the card while in the States. But Dad had died years ago.

Later that week in Harare chills went up my spine when I heard the gruesome details of a mother and daughter who had died on that same stretch of road. They, too, were returning from a school holiday, a day after us, and they were also overtaking a bus, which ended up on top of their car. A friend happened to pass the scene and saw the twisted remains of both vehicles. Then, a couple nights later in our African home, I woke to use the toilet. As I entered our unlit bathroom, as if in a bizarre night vision, I saw a creature rush across the floor at my feet.

A SNAKE!

Jumping about like an Olympic gold medalist, I grabbed a long stick. With my body tense and my fists clenched, fury churned in my gut. I beat that serpent's head, beating it as if it were the culprit behind our razor-close escape from death. When I finished, it lay there, curled up in death, and with a broom I swept it out of our house.

In Africa, our world seemed at times to obviously overlap with an invisible realm of malevolent forces, manifesting in people and situations. It was not a fight against visible enemies but against evil, spiritual forces as real as flesh and blood. "The thief," Jesus said, "comes only to steal, kill, and destroy." I saw in Africa the reality of that thief: sickness, accidents, heartache. I pondered how many times over a twenty-two-year period God had spared us from the Destroyer. I had learned, therefore, to find strength in Christ and exercise spiritual authority during times of demonic confusion and fear. My first year back from Zimbabwe, I continued to thank God, imagining that we were safe now, living in America, the land of safety and security.

And now Ethan is killed in a "freak accident"?

My mind replays the whirling of the hammer thrower, and Ethan standing with friends in the distance. The steel device is launched and goes flying through the air. There are shouts. There is movement. The sixteen-pound hammer speeds toward the group of boys at sixty miles an hour. But this time, God's hand steadies Ethan, and the instrument of death misses him, and the Grim Reaper is denied its victim just as he was not allowed to touch us in Africa.

Turning onto the bridge, I cross the Little Miami River. It's hard to believe that I'm coming home from my son's funeral. Pat didn't like calling it a "Home Going." She preferred to just call it a memorial.

The Bible calls the devil "the prince of the power of the air."

I was told that moments before Ethan was struck, a paper bag blew across Lawson Field, and Ethan turned to Elliot, saying, "Reminds me of the Dementors coming." I Googled *Harry Potter* and found a scene in which the wind blows papers across a field and the Dementors come. They are evil beings that roam the earth; they glory in decay and despair, draining people of peace and hope, devouring happiness out of the very air.

Did Ethan's words precipitate the attack? Did he somehow give Satan permission?

Satan must have been allowed to strike for a reason greater than what Ethan said, for he is powerless to hurt us unless God allows it.

Ethan told a teammate at Wheaton College, "I am willing to die for the Lord."

Before his death, Jesus said, "Every day I was with you in the temple courts and you did not lay a hand on me. But this is your hour—when darkness reigns" (Luke 22:53, NIV).

Jesus realized Satan was permitted to act against him, and he knew his Father permitted it for a greater purpose, our eternal redemption. But it must have been excruciatingly difficult for the good angels to watch Jesus delivered into the hands of evil spirits and wicked men.

The Lord constantly protected us, all those long nights in a land of spirits. Did we somehow exhaust our allotted number of deliverances? God spared us that day on the road. He didn't allow that bus to send us down the ravine to our death. So, why allow the Evil One to strike us now? What transpired in the unseen realms to precipitate this? Was God's hedge of protection around Ethan somehow breached? Did Ethan somehow give Satan an opportunity to attack him?

Passing the Murdoch Goshen Cemetery on my left, I can't believe that tomorrow we bury Ethan in America.

I quickly look away from the cold, lifeless markers in the graveyard and back to the road.

If Ethan had lived after being hit, he could have been left in a coma or paraplegic. Some are disabled in car accidents and live in pain all their lives. Others are born with deformities—struggle all their lives.

Did God make them that way?

Everything God made was good, but he didn't create our bodies directly. We're pro-created from our parents who are genetically flawed and subject to mortality. God didn't create Alzheimer's or dementia. So, where do they come from?

Augustine explains evil as an absence of what God created. It can only exist in what was once good. It is a privation, a perversion, a parasite. It exists solely at the expense of its host. It is a corruption of good, an awful falling away from what is good. It couldn't exist without a pre-existing good and is only identifiable by way of contrasts: life contrasted with death, light with darkness, truth with lying, love with hate, knowledge with ignorance, and health with disease.

In the case of Ethan's death, it was an absence of safety. It was a lack of rules, deficient equipment, inadequate training. It was a hole in the supervision and oversight. Safety was missing somewhere in the protocol for the hammer throwing event. And on and on my mind reels as my auto pilot negotiates my way home. Finally, I turn into our driveway.

Ethan's silver Chevy sits there, unused since he died. When we moved out to the country, he had to drive an extra fifteen minutes to high school. I asked him in an apologetic tone how he felt about his new twenty-five-minute commute.

"I like the drive," he said. "It gives me time to think."

Time to think—I've had plenty of that lately.

Braking and coming to a stop, I sigh and wonder: did I hold onto my son too tightly? Did I love him more than God? Couldn't things be different than burying him tomorrow? Oh, how I wish I knew why.

· 15 ·

Ethan's Burial

....

"I want to do better."

....

ON SLOPING GREEN HILLS stand concrete crosses, white statues of angels, and the sculpture of a woman weeping over her beloved. Granite stone memorials mark the names, birthdays, and death-days of those who lie beneath the ground at Saint Joseph's Cemetery. A few were buried recently and remembered; most were laid to rest long ago and forgotten, their mourners now occupying graves nearby.

It's 10:27 a.m.

A black hearse idles in front of us, and behind us is a line of waiting cars. Family members stand outside their cars in small clusters and talk. I get out of Elesha's car. Dark clouds shroud the sun; moisture is in the air. I'm met with hugs and unspoken expressions of grief.

Walking to the hearse, I see through its back windows the silver casket holding Ethan's body. It fills the rear compartment. Visualizing my boy's body lying in that box, I open and close my eyes rapidly to fight back a torrent of feelings and a floodgate of tears. The driver's tinted window glides down, revealing an older man from Meyer and

Geiser Funeral Home. Again, I put on a brave face as I prepare to do what was unimaginable eight days ago.

"Our families are here. We'll follow you down now to the burial plot."

The procession slowly descends a knoll and follows a bend around to the left. We park along an asphalt road. The funeral home director opens the back of the hearse and carefully positions the pallbearers. They bear the casket off the rollers and out of the hearse, smoothly balancing the weight. Pat and I lead our families onto the grass and between a row of tombstones. The pallbearers maneuver behind us along an adjacent row, bit by bit. Pat and I arrive at a freshly dug hole in the ground with a canopy overhead.

Moving to the far side, at the top of the grave, I try to swallow the lump in my throat while I watch Mom slowly make her way, struggling with her walker on the uneven grass. My brother, Carmen, and sister, Mary Ann, walk beside her to offer support. I glance again at Mom's name engraved on the headstone nearby: Anella 'Dolly' Roser, July 28, 1924-. She has outlived her siblings and everyone she grew up with. Now, at ninety-two, she must witness the burial of her youngest grandchild. All of life has gone haywire.

The pallbearers lift Ethan's casket onto a golden metal rack with a clink.

My son, how can I bury you? You were meant to bury me!

Ethan is suspended above the only remaining family plot, next to my dad. Our families last gathered on this spot twenty years ago, to the very month, in May 1997. We had come from Africa for Ethan's birth. Held in Pat's womb that rainy day we laid Dad to rest, Ethan was alive. When we buried Dad, I wished Ethan could've met his grandfather. But Dad died two months before he was born.

On the opposite side of the hole in the ground, Mom and our extended families gather around Pat and me. I look across at Pat's sister, Mary Margret. A couple of days ago, she reminded me of a dream she had last Christmas. In it, Ethan was dressed in white, fur handsome. His agile legs suddenly and gracefully spring into action. He skips along into the wooded area of our property adjacent to the road. His beauty and freedom touch my soul.

"Reminds me of Ethan," I say to Pat, "the way he happily played in the yard."

Two hours later, I'm driving up the hill on our street, and I can't believe what I see.

"Oh, Jesus!" I exclaim—the young deer lies in the road, dead—a car must've just hit him.

Why didn't they stop? People are always in a hurry. They fly down this road! Why doesn't someone move his body?

Oh, God, now I've got to drag him off the road. But I don't want to do it. Somebody must. I can't let him be run over again.

Did he suffer long?

I try to see where the poor animal was hit.

I don't even get him off the road before I sob like the bursting of flood gates giving way, and I make loud sounds I've never made before.

Why did this happen when I was coming down the road?

Taking deep breaths, I make it home and retreat to my office, trying to calm myself. That deer must have traumatized me. He must have tapped into a sea of sorrow. Moments ago, he freely skipped about in our yard, and now he's blindsided.

Life is cruel.

No, it's death that is cruel! It's the ultimate brutality.

On my bookshelf, *The Meditations of St. Augustine* remind me that the evil in the world did not originate with God. It has no place in him. Augustine's logic argues, if I could heal the deer's wound, it doesn't mean that the wound dwells elsewhere. No, that wound would cease to exist, because a wound is not a substance, but a defect in the fleshly substance. It is an absence of health. In the same way, what we call vices in the soul are but absences of goodness, and when they are cured, they are not transferred elsewhere but cease to exist. Augustine doesn't and she heard Pat say, "Ethan is going to accept a position at the Vineyard." But in her dream, I said, "No, Ethan will go where God tells him." Mary Margret had asked Ethan if he had a white suit. He said, "No." She said, "Ethan, I never dream about you," and she told him her dream. Ethan didn't say anything; he just looked very serious. The funeral home asked me if we had clothes we wanted Ethan buried in or if they should simply dress him in a white gown. "Put him in a white gown," I told them.

When Ethan was small, I often prayed for his future. On one occasion, I felt God say to me, "Ethan will be a minister par excellence." So I expected him to serve God to a ripe old age. But God doesn't always do things the way we imagine. From what I've heard from his friends, Ethan was already an example of ministry excellence.

As we stand around Ethan's grave, I share these thoughts and quote John 12:24 (NIV): "Truly, I tell you, unless a kernel of wheat falls to the ground and dies, it remains only a single seed. But if it dies, it produces many seeds."

Nathan then reads from Romans chapter five, while I stare at this hole in the ground next to my dad's grave. Fathers precede us, and in grief we expect to bury them. But today, I bury all the generations to come through my son.

Johnathan says a prayer of committal, and we return to our cars. We decided beforehand we could not bear to watch Ethan's casket lowered into the ground.

Later, at the house, I toss the mail on my desk. I need to meet Tom Kelly and give him Ethan's shoes and clothes to take on his trip to Zimbabwe.

"Come," Pat says, finding me in the garage. "There's a young deer outside our bedroom."

From our bedroom window, we watch the creature lower his head to feed. He then turns around to look, and I wonder if he can hear us or if he senses someone is watching. His tail is pure white, his brownish-gray claim that the evil in the world, natural or moral, is unreal, for mere nothingness cannot bear bad fruit or aggressively replicate itself like a virus. His point is that evil is not a thing God created, but a lostness of the good God made when he created the world.

God gave people power over the earth and its creatures. Since sin and death entered the world, the whole of creation is subject to this ugly futility. Creation itself longs to be rescued from the curse of thorns and decay, and its deliverance is directly connected to our redemption. Someday, the lion and the lamb will lie down together, and a little child will lead them. Oh, what a world that will be! There'll be no harm or destruction in the earth (Romans 8:19–23; Isaiah 11:6–9).

How far afield we've gone from that. How odd that I said of that deer, "He reminds me of Ethan," and now he lies on the side of the road— dead. Why did that happen? Did my words cause his demise? Is the devil out to torment me?

What's going on?

Trying to take my mind off this madness all around me, I open the mail on my desk.

A letter from Dallas Baptist University, Steve Mullen, Dean: "The beginning of each semester, from now on I will tell Ethan's story, express how fragile life is and explain that I will visit with each student about his faith. Because I knew about Ethan's faith, his legacy will live on at DBU."

How thoughtful! They seemed so organized at DBU. Would such an accident have happened there? Would Ethan still be alive if he stayed at DBU? Would have he died some other way? The how question assaults me again. Daily, the one-two punch of the how-why beats me up.

Another letter I open is typed on Wheaton College's stationery.

Is it about their insurance?

No!

From Carla Lovett, Department of History: "Faculty always have a few students throughout their careers who are more special. Ethan was one of those for me. He started the semester slowly, as is the case of most transfer students, but he came to me and apologized for his performance, saying, 'I want to do better.' Students frequently make promises of this sort with little or nothing coming out of it. However, Ethan made good on his. He finished with perfect attendance, contributed thoughtfully to every discussion, completed all reading assignments, and got the highest grade out of two classes on his last exam. I was absolutely thrilled Ethan lived up to his commitment, that his character was truly as solid as it seemed. Little did I know that on Saturday he would . . ."

Wheaton is a top Christian school, among the best liberal arts colleges in the nation. When Ethan wanted to transfer, I couldn't argue with their credentials. But I can't stop thinking about that fateful day and how my boy died there.

I must respond to their email about the NCAA insurance.

> Dear Paul,
> We appreciate your prayers.
> I have received an outline of the policies that you feel may apply and may provide benefits to us. I also understand your intention to pursue these claims vigorously with the insurance carriers on our behalf. . . .

Should I do it?

My typing stops and I feel my heart beating faster. The cursor flashes on the screen. It bids me to return where I left off as if it's impatient with the course of action I'm deliberating. But I've heard nothing more from Wheaton since that lone email, and that was two weeks ago.

Saving my email to Paul in my drafts folder, I flip through the recent letters I've received from lawyers in Chicago: a high-gloss packet, a full-color picture of three men in suits, and a third with a folder packed with information and a DVD titled "Wrongful Deaths." Each mailing has a cover letter expressing sympathy for our loss and asking me to contact them. But I'm not interested in firms with glossy ads.

I do a search for a lawyer on Avvo, an online marketplace for legal services. David Schwaner's review stands out. "He did what he said he would do." I email Schwaner and ask him what he thinks about how the accident happened, and if he's willing to have a look at Wheaton's email and let me know what he thinks about it. Then I reopen my draft to Paul.

> Being unlearned in these matters, and acting in the best interest of Ethan's legacy, I made an initial contact today with a lawyer to advise us on these matters.

That'll get them to respond!

Now they'll know I'm serious, and I imagine President Ryken phoning me to ask how they can resolve the matter. They can't just leave us with Ethan was told not to turn his back. No, I can't live with that for the rest of my life.

· 16 ·

What Do I Do Now?

....

"You really are my best friends!"

....

TWO MORE WEEKS GO BY, and I can't believe Wheaton hasn't responded to my red flag.

What do I do now?

In Africa, I once contacted a lawyer on $15,000 I was owed, but after paying $2,000 in legal fees, I could see it was going to be like Charles Dickens's *Bleak House*. But shoot, if the school shows no concern about my involving a lawyer, why should I?

Why not phone the lawyer in Chicago and hear what he has to say?

"I read Wheaton's email to you," David Schwaner says. "They're not sure if the NCAA policies apply to Ethan since he wasn't a participant in the event."

"Why don't they respond to my email?"

"They may not without a lawyer. I've sent a retainer agreement and a form to release health information on your son."

What about my good Christian testimony?

My body tenses up, imagining the headlines, "Missionary Sues Christian College," and finally I say, "I saw those forms in my inbox, but we don't want to sue the school."

I've never sued anyone. When a woman ran into me in the rain and punctured my fender, I simply asked her to send our mission a donation. I didn't want her insurance to go up.

"I understand your feelings," David says, "but having a lawyer doesn't mean you are suing them. . . ."

A few hours later, Nathan, Perry, Pat, and I are sitting in a restaurant. Nathan's wife, Perry, is lovely, very petite, wearing a pretty dress. Nathan has on a long-sleeved, checkered, button-up shirt. For years, Ethan wore the clothes Nathan passed down to him. You couldn't tell them apart in their pictures from age five to ten. The waiter comes with water and we order dinner.

Then the words slide out of my mouth: "I contacted a lawyer."

As soon as I say it, I regret not telling Nathan privately. I grip my glass of water. *But oh, God, I'm tired of waiting.*

"Why did you do that?" he asks, leaning forward on the table.

"I need to know what happened" I set my glass down. "It's just not right."

"No, Dad, it's on the school to do what's right. Not for us to have a lawyer threaten them."

Perry turns and looks at Nathan while Pat shifts her body toward me.

"They've not responded to my email, and that was two weeks ago."

"Why are you doing this?" Nathan asks, his voice probing.

"My son DIED!" My intensity surprises me.

"He was MY brother," Nathan answers, his voice rising.

Employees from behind the counter eye us with questioning looks, and two tables of customers look over in our direction.

"I WANTED his advice." I can't help myself now; something erupts inside of me. "We're NOT obligated to do anything. I just made an initial contact to see what a lawyer thought!"

Perry's eyes widen and under the table Pat's knee knocks against mine. Their body language shouts, "Guys, take it down a few notches."

But I'm angry, and my anger feels easier to manage than my grief. But why say anything more? You've told him. Now, just shut up!

The waiter brings our food. "If you need anything else," he says, "just let me know." His voice sounds nervous, but his face has a curious look as if he knows something about what we're arguing over. Perhaps he read the articles in the paper and recognizes us.

Nathan and I eat in silence. I might as well eat gravel. Nothing satisfies me, no matter how much I eat. It only quiets the rumbling for a while and is of little comfort. Pat and Perry make small talk while I finish what's on my plate.

Standing up, I put on my jacket and pay the cashier.

In the parking lot, Pat and I hug Nathan and Perry, and we say goodbye.

Pat shuts her car door and asks, "Why did you say anything to Nathan?"

"You're right," I reply. "I shouldn't have said anything."

"I don't want you two arguing. Can't you deal with Wheaton without involving him?"

"I will need to tell Nathan sooner or later if we hire a lawyer."

I've always been open with my sons. I value their input.

"Are you going to hire a lawyer?"

"I don't know. Wheaton is not giving me much of an option."

Now Pat can't leave it alone, and I don't want to say anything more.

"We must get on with our lives!" she emphatically declares.

My anger surges and I decide to let my feelings rip.

"You WILL NOT," I scream as loud as I can, "tell me how to grieve my son's death—and I will not tell you how to grieve!"

I look from the road to her shocked face.

"Okay," she says. "I'm sorry. I will not tell you how to grieve."

While we drive the rest of the way up Route 48, Pat doesn't say anything, and I don't want to say anything. A bottleneck of feelings, a warehouse of thoughts, are all turned upside down in me like garbage cans strewn all about or trash on the side of the road.

As I turn onto Murdoch Goshen Road, it is like I can hear Pat's mind ticking.

When I turn down our driveway, she softly says in a questioning sort of way, "Ethan would've been home today. . . ."

"Yeah," I groan, and I hate the harsh new reality of an empty house.

As I pull to a stop alongside Ethan's Cavalier, it refuses to be ignored. "No, he's not here. But I am!" It will not be silent. "He would've been here if it weren't for that freak accident." It mocks me, "No, he's never coming home."

As I turn the car off, Pat looks across at me caringly and says, "I was so looking forward to Ethan coming home this summer. I didn't have as much time with him as you did, taking him to his soccer."

I sit silent, motionless, my heart aching. I'm also not ready to go inside.

"And now, there's no more time," Pat says. "No time to express love. The routines of life are gone, never to be reclaimed. So many lost opportunities."

I shouldn't have pushed her grief button or there'll be two of us elegiac. But the house itself looks as if it mourns. It is dark and distant, like a stranger—no greeting, just a blank stare.

"Spring break was the last time I saw Ethan," Pat says. "I hemmed his coat before he rushed out the door. 'Mom, don't worry,' he said. 'It's okay.' But I wanted to do it. He gave me a big hug on the porch. 'I gotta go. I'm meeting someone on the way out of town.' Then, he tenderly said, 'I love you, Mom.'" As she says it, her voice breaks.

What can I now say to ease her pain?

I push the garage door remote; the door moans as it opens, stopping with an abrupt clank.

Pat follows me inside the kitchen, and I flip all three sets of lights on.

My anger is gone, and I put my arm around Pat while memories of coming home through that door stir my heart.

"Last summer," I say, "while we were away, Ethan saw a mouse running around."

"He knew I was upset when I saw their droppings," Pat says, "but he told me anyway."

"Ethan didn't like mice either," Pat adds, as she brushes a tear away and sets her purse down on the kitchen island.

"You remember when I gave him five dollars to get a play mouse and we put it on your pillow?" I ask. " 'Come in the bedroom when Mom comes out of the bathroom,' I told him. Act like you're saying goodnight.' He put his phone on video to record your reaction."

"Yeah, when I pulled back the sheet and screamed, he busted out laughing."

"We still have that video somewhere."

I need to collect all his videos and put them in one place. There's so much I need to do. I must keep him alive. I feel my chest tighten.

At the top of the steps, Pat flips on the light that leads to Ethan's bedroom in the basement.

I should not have cursed.

"He should be here," she says. "I'm going to miss hearing him sing with his ear buds in. I'd hear him laughing, and he'd tell me, 'Oh, someone sent me a funny video.' "

As I retreat to my office, I can't help noticing in the hallway that we're all smiles in both our sons' wedding pictures. We laughed and danced. But now happiness has deserted us. It's so far from us, as if never to return. He in whom we had long delighted is gone. What will we do? He made our house a home. Now it feels like a mausoleum. He will never come into our bedroom and say, "Good night." He will never sit on our bed again and say, "You really are my best friends!" I don't know if I can still live here!

He helped me live upright.

Later that night, I wake from a dream. Ethan is in the lower level, searching through the boxes he took to college, trying to find something. *What's he looking for?* I ask myself in anguish. *What has he lost?*

I wake up and go down the steps to Ethan's room. I know he's not there, but I go anyway.

As his summer vacation approached, he said, "I'll see you in three and a half weeks."

"I hope they go fast!" I replied.

Switching the light on, I stare at his pictures on the wall, his handwritten notes on his desk, his soccer ball on the floor, and his trophies on the shelf, all sitting where he left them. His bed sheets are fresh and folded back, a soft comforter at the foot of his bed.

I can't take it any longer. I kneel on the floor next to his bed and weep.

"I want my son BACK!" I howl.

In the morning, my first conscious thoughts again: It's true. It really happened. He died. Then, feelings of dread and shock come over me. For days now, that reality has overwhelmed me each morning when I wake. There's an empty place in my heart he once filled, a huge void in my world nothing else can fill. With gnawing grief, today, I start another day, and I hear myself saying it again. "I can't believe it happened!"

I know I mustn't keep saying that. It only perpetuates my feelings of alarm and panic. But I find it hard to stop.

·17·

"Not Paying Attention"

"Growing up as a third culture kid on the mission field instilled in me a common sense of responsibility."

MONDAY, MAY 22. Exactly a month ago, Ethan died in the early evening.

As I drive to the library this morning, thoughts assail me: *I should've visited him that day!* I would've made sure he was safe. Why did that other parent take her son that day, and I didn't take Ethan? *Why did he agree to do a double shift?* He should not have been there.

I imagine turning the clock back, traveling in a time machine to thirty days ago. Yes, we would do that day over again. I would drive to Chicago and take him with me early that morning. He wouldn't volunteer for the track meet, because I've booked a special surprise for him. I take him somewhere he's never been before. We go out of town. Drive north to Crystal Lake or south to Kankakee. Anywhere but Wheaton, Illinois. We are as far from Lawson Field as we can get—miles away, out of reach.

We book extravagant all-day events. We spend money like there's no tomorrow. I tell him how much I love him and how special he is to our family. And he is not on that field when those hammers are thrown. If a hammer is destined to hit somebody, Ethan does not see it or hear about it till the next day. Our events necessitate our phones being turned off. And he has no regrets about coming back from the joys of heaven because he's never been there.

He's here with me.

At Symmes Library, I turn on my laptop to write more of Ethan's story and a music file opens: "Can't Say Goodbye."

Now how did that get there? I never listen to music on this laptop! I hit the file and a message box opens: "The shortcut item, 'Can't Say Goodbye.mp3,' has been changed or moved. Do you want to delete this shortcut? Yes/No"

NO!

I Google the song. It's from an album called *Redemption.* The lyrics: "Sometimes, I think that I can make it. But most days, well, I get by on faking, Cause I won't let them see me cry. . . . Late at night, your name is calling. . . . But there's no way you can now. I wish there was a way somehow. So, I will remember you. And I will hold you close there in my heart and never let you go. . . . Lord, tell me how is this fair. When in his eyes, I see your memory there."

Uninvited tears seize me. I clutch my laptop and head for a private cubicle.

Why did that song come up now? I've used this laptop for six months. *Ethan had it last year when he was still doing our worship songs at church.*

My cell phone vibrates. Mary Ann, my sister's name, comes up on my screen.

"Have you seen the article in the *Chicago Tribune*?" she asks.

"No," I whisper, turning my laptop off. "I'm inside the library."

"Well, I didn't want to trouble you, but the *Tribune* has an article online: 'A Moment of Inattention Cost Wheaton College Student Ethan Roser His Life.' They're quoting the police."

"The police report on the accident must have just been filed, but that's a horrible headline!" I jam my stuff in a bag and head for the door.

"The reporter is John. Do you want to talk to him? Or should I phone them for you?"

"Leave it for now. When I get home, I'll read his article."

When I get inside the door at home, I hear the phone ringing in my office. I quickly pick it up.

"Hi, this is John Keilman of the *Chicago Tribune*. I'm very sorry about your son. We are planning on doing a follow-up article on the accident, and we wanted to reach out to you."

"Not paying attention," I blurt out, "wasn't the reason my son died. Everyone, officials included, thought he and the other boys were safe. Ethan was the farthest out of bounds. I just want you to get the facts right."

"I was just quoting Detective Uhlir. I can update the electronic version."

That evening, the headline remains unchanged:

> "Police: Inattention cost Wheaton College student Ethan Roser his life when he was hit in the head by an errant hammer throw," Wheaton police Detective Andrew Uhlir said. Roser, 19, was struck when he was standing with two others about 30 feet outside the in-bound landing area. . . . Uhlir said the official overseeing the event, a Moody Bible Institute professor whom the detective would not name, didn't believe anything was amiss. From the official's statement, he saw where these three individuals were, and he felt they were in a safe position. And based on where they were, they felt they were in a safe position. He noted that the NCAA track and field rule book does not provide guidance about where volunteers should stand during the

hammer throw. Uhlir said that during warmups, two of the volunteers were goofing off with a stick used to mark the throws. Roser was watching the horseplay when the hammer struck him. The weight barely missed another volunteer and, after striking Roser, continued on to hit another young man in the head, causing minor injuries. Uhlir said the volunteers had been told that they needed to keep their focus on the throwers. . . . College officials did not respond to a request for comment. Roser had actually finished his assigned shift for the meet before the fatal throw but had stuck around to cover for a teammate who was visiting with family members.

(John Keilman, *Chicago Tribune,* May 22, 2017)

"God, this isn't right!" I shout. "Now they're blaming the victim." And of course, the school has no comment.

I'm mad at the *Chicago Tribune.* I'm mad at the police. I'm mad at the school. I'm mad at the NCAA.

The next morning, I'm still angry.

Papers around the country have picked up the story. The Associated Press headline in all caps reads: "POLICE: STUDENT KILLED BY HAMMER THROW DIDN'T PAY ATTENTION."

This is utter nonsense, but more articles than I dare read are coming up on my screen blaming Ethan. The initial reports spoke of Ethan's faith in Christ and his wholesome character, and now a lie presents him as an irresponsible person, and they broadcast this lie all over the world.

Our son's life was violently taken and then he gets blamed. What parent would allow that?

I take a deep breath and dial Detective Uhlir's number off the business card he gave me.

"Detective Uhlir, Wheaton Police Department."

"Hi, I'm Mark Roser, Ethan Roser's father. It's extremely difficult for us to hear you say that Ethan died because he was not paying attention. I'm on a CapTel phone due to hearing loss. There's a delay on my side before your words appear on my screen. So, please be patient with me."

There is a long pause.

"Okay. The media tends to put things the way they want. They can spin the words to make it interesting for a reader. But in no way, shape, or form is the bottom line that your son was not paying attention. That's one factor of many, and although those words are associated with me, it's not what I said. I simply related all the facts to him."

"You can check Ethan's license. He drove since he was sixteen and never had a moving or parking violation, not one ticket. Does that sound like a boy who doesn't pay attention?"

"I apologize for what you have read and the anguish this has caused you. The accident could have been avoided on many, many different levels. If there's some way I can help . . ."

"That's why I'm calling. Would you call John Keilman at the *Tribune* and tell him that he misquoted you? Correct this blaming of the victim?"

"We don't get involved in what the media says. They do what they want with what we tell them. But personally, I think there should be a horn blown before each throw. You can't have a sixteen-pound steel weight traveling over a hundred feet in the air to an area where people are standing without some kind of warning. And if people are there to bring the hammers back during warmups, why not buy more hammers and wait until the warmup throws are finished? It is worth a child's life! That is my opinion, but I don't include my opinions in a report."

But the paper sure attributes opinions to you!

Since he'll not phone the *Tribune*, I'll phone David, the lawyer, and see if he can get the paper or police to clear my son's name.

"At this point, it's best to deal with the school," David says. "I talked to Larry Judge. He's an expert on the hammer throw. He did a report a few years ago on safety concerns for the event. 'There's an urgent need to increase the height of cages and width of gates. Otherwise,' he wrote in his report, 'schools and the NCAA risk a catastrophic accident and a lawsuit.' But the new specifications were not adopted."

"Why not?"

"I guess they didn't want to spend the money. But, Mark, I also found that the man who supervised the event isn't certified by the NCAA."

"Does the NCAA require hammer throw officials to be certified?"

"No."

"That's crazy! They require baseball umpires and football refs to be certified, and those sports are far less dangerous than the hammer throw!"

"The NCAA protocol for the whole event is too loose," David says.

"What kind of training did Ethan have? What does the NCAA require?"

"I talked to Mark Heckel, another expert. He said they don't require any training."

"No safe cage, no certified officials, no training of volunteers. It sounds like a case of the blind leading the blind, and we end up in the pit!"

"Exactly. You need to know that your son's death was not his fault. . . ."

I must get out of this house.

Taking my blue zip-up jacket off a hanger, I am gripped with intense sadness the moment I touch it. I wore this in Chicago. Does my mind recall wearing it during those dreadful days, or does it carry sorrow in its very fibers, like a shirt saturated with sweat?

At Lowe's, I buy a filter for our air conditioner unit since the weather is warming up and I haven't changed it in Lord knows how long.

As I come out of the store, a car speeds by me, missing me by only a few feet. An older woman at the crosswalk also looks shocked by this guy's recklessness. If either of us had hurried to our cars like he was hurrying, he would've hit us. I watch him fly noisily onto the street. I'm boiling inside. I want to confront him. I envision myself jumping into my car and catching up with him at a red light.

The scene vividly unfolds in my imagination like a sleepless dream. . . .

"Man, what's wrong with you? You are driving like a nut!" He pulls out a gun and shakes it at me. "Okay, mister," I say, "let's see you use that thing!" And I refuse to back down. Boom—the last thing I hear is the sound of the gun going off.

Since Ethan died, I have felt the pull of death. It has a hand on me. Departing this world is appealing. I would be with Christ and with Ethan. The world, its trappings, its thrills, its attachments are no longer attractive. My happy temperament lies buried beneath the ground. My heart is gone, my body is empty, like his, and rigor mortis has taken hold of me.

I've had to learn to cope with tinnitus. But now, how do I manage this grief? I know tinnitus can cause depression, post-traumatic stress, anxiety, anger, and suicide. It's the first and largest category of disability in the military; hearing loss is a close second and PTSD third.

Ethan's death has caused me to ask, "Is it better to die, than to live? And if this life has more advantages than dying, why did my son die?"

Didn't Moses ask to die because of his troubles? And Job, and Jeremiah, and Jonah? Even Elijah, after his victory at Mount Carmel, asked to die. Then there's Paul, who best justifies my death wish. "I desire to depart and be with Christ, which is better by far," he writes from prison (Philippians 1:23 NIV). Yes, if he dies, he goes to heaven to be with his Savior. Who would blame him? Also, Paul wanted to know why a messenger of Satan was permitted to buffet him. That demon made his life miserable (2 Corinthians 12:7).

When I had talked of buying a burial plot, Elesha cried. "You have to play with my children." Sure, I'd like to walk her down the aisle, play with my grandchildren, know Pat is taken care of, see my sons established in the ministry, and know that God's call on my life is fulfilled; yet, in seeing how expendable Ethan was, I think God doesn't need me here to do anything.

Only the drive to write Ethan's story gets me out of bed in the morning.

"Oh, God, get me through today," I say each morning. At night, lying in bed. "Thank you for getting me through today!"

Back at the house that evening, I'm contemplating what to do about these false reports when I get a news alert in my inbox:

> Who's to blame for hammer-throw death? Ethan Roser was laughing with friends. A minute later, there was so much blood gushing out of his mouth no one could perform mouth-to-mouth resuscitation. They were standing outside the field of play. "Just being kids," one student later explained to police. Then, an errant throw . . . Thud. Crunch. Those were the words witnesses used to describe the sound that reverberated around Lawson Field at Wheaton College. The hammer hit Roser just as he looked up. The 19-year-old fell to the ground and didn't move. "I think I just hit someone," the thrower from Aurora University said, before walking off the field to hug his brother. Police said he was visibly upset, telling them it was an accident. Roser was bleeding out of his mouth and nose. A parent of another athlete rushed over and saw part of his skull. He tried to move Roser, but blood pooled into his left ear. Roser's chest moved up and down, but with every breath, more blood streamed out his mouth. While one person pumped his chest, another swept the blood out of his mouth. His faint pulse soon couldn't be found. He was turning blue. . . .

"Oh, dear God!" I wail and lie on the floor, sobbing. The trauma of Ethan's death hits me all over again, this time with lethal force.

Must I experience this pain every day of my life? I shouldn't have read that article. *Pat and Elesha must never read it!*

We agreed not to look at the pictures the police took and included in their report. I never want to see Ethan like that again because how do you get those images out of your mind? With strong tears, I try to wash away Ethan's devastated face and crushed skull. And I understand why the Bible says, "Abel's blood cried out from the ground!"

· 18 ·

God Grieves

*"Imagine the pain the God who literally created
our emotional spectrum feels when we say we love him
and still choose the crap he hates. We have the
emotional capacity of a twig compared to God,
and it hurts me to see people who say they love him
but are knowingly content in sin."*

SUNDAY AT CHURCH, the lead female vocalist smiles broadly as she leads the congregation, swaying her shoulders and singing the words, "What can wash away my sin?"

And we all merrily answer in the song, "Nothing but the blood of Jesus!"

The word "blood" hits me sideways, and I stop singing.

Two male guitarists strum away and provide backup vocals, singing and smiling, while a drummer pounds away behind a see-through cage.

I look around the church. Everybody in the place is smiling as they sing. "What can make me whole again?"

There is a pause and then, "Nothing but the blood of Jesus!"

The blood—and again I see that metal hammer strike Ethan's head. "Nothing but the blood!"

My son coughs violently for two to three minutes, struggling in his attempt to clear his airways of blood. But there's too much of it to breathe. It pours out of him.

"Oh! Precious is the flow."

And I stand there, powerless, and witness his life blood gushing out of his mouth and ears onto the ground, and I see a crack in his skull.

"For my pardon, this I see. Nothing but the blood of Jesus!"

A scene from *The Passion of the Christ* replays in my mind's eye: metal and bones tied to leather strands tear open Jesus' skin, exposing his veins, arteries and intestines. Mary crawls on her hands and knees with a cloth, weeping as she wipes her son's blood off the pavement. Somber music plays in the background. Blood is everywhere.

Everyone but me is swaying to the words and happily singing, "No other fount I know."

How many pints of blood poured from Jesus' body while his Father watched?

"Nothing but the blood of Jesus!"

I've never thought much about rejoicing in Jesus' bleeding, and I mumble to myself, "The death of God's Son was far more violent and gruesome than my son's death," while delighted sinners sing, "This is all my hope and peace. Nothing but the blood of Jesus."

The more you love someone, the greater the anguish in watching them suffer and die—and the Father watched his Son writhe in pain and heard his derelict cry, as for the first time ever, the Son of his love felt utterly abandoned and God-forsaken. I hear Jesus cry from the cross, "My God, my God, why have you forsaken me?" The Son had been in the bosom of the Father since before time began, but now, the separating power of death pierced the Godhead.

"This is all my righteousness. Nothing but the blood of Jesus."

Jesus was a man like me, and his body and soul were made desolate. It's a killer when the one you love abandons you. Did he die of a broken heart? Was his grief so intense that it ruptured his heart? Jesus' suffering and the Father's love in offering up his Son for me takes on a deeper, more personal meaning.

"I get it," I say. Tears well up in my eyes.

"Good morning!" the pastor booms from the mic, and all the room lights are switched on.

You must compose yourself. He's going to tell us to greet someone.

"Please be seated," he says. "We're going to celebrate the Lord's Table today. Remembering and proclaiming Jesus' death for us!"

We sit and ushers stand. I hear myself exhale and hope no one hears me.

"Imagine the pain the God who literally created our emotional spectrum feels," Ethan had tweeted, "when we say we love him and still choose the crap he hates."

More than once, Ethan asked me how he could help his friends who claimed to be Christians, and yet got drunk and had casual sex.

Hosea says, "When Israel was a child, I loved him. . . . [But] they sacrificed to the Baals and burned incense to carved images. I taught Ephraim to walk, taking them by their arms. But they did not know that I healed them. I drew them with gentle cords, with bands of love. . . . I stooped and fed them. . . . [But] my people are bent on backsliding from Me. . . . How can I give you up? . . . My heart churns within Me. My compassion is stirred" (11:1–8).

"God so loved the world," the pastor says, "that he gave his only begotten Son."

How amazing is God's love?

In the Song of Solomon, it's compared to an earnest suitor. He opens his heart to woo her, but she shuts the door on him. "The Lovesick God," I called my series of messages, and I referred to the prophet Hosea because our indifference to God's love strikes his heart like the nails that pierced Jesus' hands and feet. In the end, he gives his life to her and wins her wayward heart once and for all. Thoughts of God suffering touch the innermost cords of my heart and draw me near to him.

There is no other way!

On the far side of our aisle, an usher appears with a basket of crackers. The basket comes down our row, and I take a cracker, clutching it in my palm.

"Instead of Ethan," a Wheaton parent wrote me, "it could have been any of our boys!" Before that day, it always was someone else's boy. And I never took the awful grief home.

Another usher appears with a tray of small communion cups in a tray holder.

What of God's pain and sorrow? The first time grief is found in the Bible, it's God who grieves. Yet, we hear so very little of God's grief. Before the Great Flood, "God's heart was full of pain," because humankind had filled the earth with violence (Genesis 6:6, NIrv). And his heart broke like the earth's great depths that broke in a thousand places, and for days on end, his tears flooded the earth.

The tray is passed, carefully, down our row. I take a cup and steady it in my hand.

When did I last grieve over the hurt that I've caused God?

The pastor holds up the cracker. "Jesus said, 'My body, broken for you.'"

I place the cracker in my mouth and chew.

"Jesus wept" is the shortest verse in the Bible. Again, in Gethsemane, he wept "with loud crying" the writer to the Hebrews says. Isaiah names the Messiah "Man of Sorrows, acquainted with grief."

"Christ's blood," the pastor says, "shed for the remission of your sins."

It is enough!

I drink the warm juice. Jesus' sinless soul willingly offered up in place of my sinful soul. The perfect life, which should not have

ended, was cut off so that my messed-up life might continue. The
Father freely delivered his only Son over to death. His blood speaks
forgiveness and mercy. The Holy Spirit, in his dealings with me, now
suffers patiently to make me holy. How it must hurt God to hear
people mock his Son and use his name as a curse word.

And who comforts God when he grieves?

After one news article, a comment from a reader made fun of Ethan
for not paying attention. He joked about how "he got hammered at
college." Another belittled his death as if he was "stupid." Someone
also questioned my love for Ethan because I said, "It comforts us to
know that our son is in heaven."

The ushers appear again, and row by row they collect our empty
cups.

Soon thereafter, on a Monday, a package arrives: three books from
my sister, Mary Ann. Since I'm writing Ethan's story, one interests
me right away: *Getting Grief Right: Finding Your Story of Love in the
Sorrow of Loss.*[2] This book looks far better than the one on grief that
I'm reading, which advises me to "Identify who you are, independent
of your deceased loved one. If you lost a child, are you still their
parent?" That cut my tattered heart. I now pull that book out of my
laptop bag and stick it on the bookshelf behind me.

What'd they know about losing a child?

The author of this new book lost his son. I'm sure he's an honest
broker. In the kitchen, grabbing my mug and a tea bag, I start the
kettle.

In the years that followed his loss, author Patrick O'Malley, a
psychotherapist, found that his grief and that of his clients didn't
match the Kübler-Ross paradigm of five stages of grief, which is so
deeply embedded in our cultural consciousness. O'Malley challenges
the idea that mourning proceeds predictably from one stage to the
next when done properly, and that grievers can expect to reach some
psychological finish line.

American culture, he argues, in pursuit of happiness, compartmentalizes mourning. Thus, mourners are advised to gauge their grief until they "get over it" or "move on," as if grief is some bad emotion that must be discarded as soon as possible. That approach, however, provides no comfort, just more pain and added anxiety. Instead, O'Malley found help in his grief and helped others in their grief by having them share the stories of the loved ones that they lost—and for me, this is just what the doctor ordered!

I take a big, long sip of my tea.

O'Malley's book also explains that people grieve differently, because no two people are alike, and no two relationships are the same. Everyone has had different experiences in life too.

Last Sunday, God opened my eyes while I was preaching. It's odd how you can live with a woman for thirty-six years and then, in an instant, you see into her heart. I had finished a difficult message in which I talked about our son's death. I looked at the pew where Pat sat alone, and I saw a bewildered three-year-old who needed assurance. I realized that the depth of my grief had frightened her and had touched on a lifetime of pain: her parents' divorce, her mother's depression and suicide, and now Ethan's death, and her husband's shattered heart. When I saw her heart, my compassion kindled in a flash, and I loved her more than ever. It was a turning point for me in our new normal, our relationship bombarded by grief, because I saw beyond my own pain. She was my partner in pain. We shared grief and had fellowship in our suffering the loss of Ethan.

"If my daughter died," a guy told me, "my wife would divorce me!"

Many marriages end after the death of a child because both individuals feel things so intensely. Conflict arises because they grieve so distinctively and deal with it so differently (women typically want to talk about it and men go quiet), or because they can't comprehend how anyone could act otherwise (moving on quickly versus camping long term), especially someone so close to them (their spouse), because they can't see past their own pain, and because their grief separates them unless real steps are taken to share their anguish at a deeper level.

We had dinner with a couple who lost their baby. I held her small dead body at the hospital and was with them when they poured her ashes into a lake. The husband consoled himself with the idea that it was selfish on his part to want his daughter to live. She needed a heart transplant, and if she survived, she was sure to struggle throughout her life. The wife, however, could not accept her baby's death. She wanted to die.

When Herod slaughtered the infants in Bethlehem, "A voice is heard in Ramah, mourning and great weeping, Rachel weeping for her children and refusing to be comforted, because they are no more" (Jeremiah 31:15, NIV).

I think it is children that keep the earth spinning. If it were not for children, I reckon the world would've ended long ago. With Ethan's death, it feels like my world has ended.

"In the hierarchy of grief," counselors say that "burying a child creates the greatest grief." Studies have also concluded that the worst grief results from the sudden, violent death of a child in their late teen years before they fully mature. Our loss fits each circumstance and throws us into the worst-case scenario. It helps to know what we are facing really is the worst. It is validating and strangely reassuring.

A week later, I open an email from Wheaton College. My heart beats faster.

> Dear Mark and Pat,
> You and your family have continued to come to our thoughts and prayers here at Wheaton. As we look to the upcoming fall semester, we are prayerfully asking the Lord for guidance in how to care for our campus community. September 1st is the first home men's soccer game, which

will mark an emotional moment for our community. Thinking back to the way you all provided gospel comfort at Ethan's funeral, I would like to invite you to come speak at chapel on Friday, September 1st.

Grace and peace,
Rev. Tim Blackmon, Chaplain
Wheaton College

I told myself, I never want to see that place again. But Chaplain Blackmon's email invitation stares at me. What would I say when I speak? And why would they ask me to speak? Blackmon says, "the way you all provided gospel comfort at Ethan's funeral."

I told the vice president, however, that I've made an initial contact with a lawyer. Blackmon must have run his invitation by the president. It's surprising they would invite me.

It would be painful to be there and to watch their soccer game. My fingers scratch my head as if it's an involuntary reflex. If I go, I'll ask the kids to go with me.

What does God want?

Johnathan phones me that evening and asks, "What did the lawyer say about Wheaton?"

"He knows we're upset about the news articles and that we want to clear Ethan's name."

"Did he have any suggestions on how we can do that?"

"The paper and police aren't going to do it. But if we file a complaint, he's confident he'll prove that Ethan was the victim, and papers across the country will pick up the story. That'll clear his name better than any other way. But he knows that we don't want to hurt the school."

"Well, we've protected the school's reputation," Johnathan says. "Did they ever follow up with you on their insurance policy? Or talk to you about what was in the papers?"

"No, just that initial email about insurance. But I did just get an invite from the chaplain to speak at chapel. Would you go with me? It's a chance to honor God and Ethan."

"Dad, we definitely want to go and do that, but Wheaton needs to take some responsibility for Ethan's death. If I were them, I would clear it up as fast as I could."

"Okay, I'm going to accept Wheaton's invitation. Who knows? Maybe they'll talk to us when we come. I know David, the lawyer in Chicago, wants to meet with us, and we could do that while we're all there."

"We need to do something!" Johnathan says.

Johnathan surprises me as much as Wheaton's invite. Our gentle giant is normally easy going. But he feels strongly that we must do something. Nathan also feels strongly that we should just leave it.

We can decide when we're together in Chicago, but I don't want this to create a rift in our family. I don't want to lose two sons.

·19·

A Chapel Service

....

"Wheaton Chapel—a place where they release chickens."

....

FRIDAY, SEPTEMBER 1, 2017, Edman Chapel. I arrange my notes at the podium. A sea of students before me, not an open seat, 2,000 undergraduates fill the ascending theater aisles and the vast horseshoe balcony. Among the young men and women present for the morning chapel are older faces too: staff, faculty, and President Ryken. On the platform sits Chaplain Blackmon, and just below the stage, Pat, Johnathan, Elesha, Nathan, and Perry.

Thousands of eyes, wondering, *What will Ethan's dad say?*

Moments before everyone poured into the auditorium, Nathan showed me a video that Ethan recorded last semester. A student released a chicken during chapel. It flapped its wings and jumped around the platform. Ethan tweeted: "Wheaton Chapel—a place where they release chickens." I told Nathan and Johnathan, "Today, I'm the chicken."

They laughed, since it's me, not them, speaking for the family. But there's no getting away from the seriousness of the mood. Steadying the microphone, I take a deep breath and look at the large clock on the back wall and then down at my notes. I've got twenty-one minutes.

The bright young faces of the students are illuminated by daylight shining through the chapel windows. They all remind me of Ethan. His friend Rilea told me, "In chapel, I whispered to Ethan, 'Listen for Bethany while we sing. She has the most beautiful voice I've ever heard.' A few chapels later, Ethan leaned over and said, 'She does have a beautiful voice!'"

He—not I—should've been here today.

Hold your emotions in check. Only say what you've prepared. Nothing about the accident, how hard it is to accept, or Ethan being blamed.

"Allow me," I say, after talking several minutes from my notes, "to share a fond memory of Ethan at age five. I had preached at a few churches, and he heard me tell a story about a donkey. So, I asked him, 'Do you want to tell it?' He smiled and nodded his head yes and held the microphone with both of his small hands.

"He spoke to the congregation with an excited voice, 'There was an old donkey that fell into a well. When he hit the bottom, he was bruised but alive. The well was dry, and the donkey brayed for help. The farmer heard the braying, but he reckoned that neither the donkey nor the well was worth saving. So, he called his neighbors and they came with their shovels to bury the donkey and fill the well. As they shoveled dirt down the well, the donkey said to himself, *This can't be happening.* The farmers, however, continued to shovel and the dirt hit the panicking donkey's back and rose up his legs. Then, a simple thought crossed his mind: *Shake it off and step up!* So, as the farmers shoveled, the donkey shook and stepped up. The faster the farmers shoveled the dirt, the faster he shook it off and stepped up.'

"By now Ethan's imitating the donkey, shaking and stepping, head going from side to side and feet up and down. The congregation was smiling at him and laughing. 'And so, the donkey rose higher and higher until he reached the top of the well. Then he stepped over the wall and walked away, free. The moral of the story is that whatever threatens to bury you has within it the capacity to lift you into a higher realm of living.'"

The students smile. They like the old donkey's story. And I'm that old donkey—a talking donkey like Balaam's jackass, a chicken thrown on stage, flapping around like crazy, shaking and stepping.

It's time to finish.

"I want to encourage you to shake off your fears and disappointments and step into your God-given calling. Ethan was doing that, and the legacy of faith I gave to my son, he gave back to me, more precious than I bestowed it." My voice cracks and I'm done.

That evening the autumn wind blows, suggesting a change of seasons, and the lights at Joe Bean Stadium brighten against the encroaching night. On a wall beyond the far goal, in white letters, "Thunder Soccer" is written on a deep blue background, blending with the evening sky.

Ethan would've been playing tonight, and it would've been Nathan and me watching him. In memory of Ethan, the team's jerseys have a patch on the shoulder that says ER. We see Erin, Coach Jake's wife, and give her notes that we wrote this afternoon for her husband. We heard he had a difficult summer. Then we sit in the grandstand near mid-field.

The next morning, we leave Harbor House and stop at Lawson Field on our way out of Wheaton. At the spot where Ethan was struck, only a small remnant of sand remains. From there, we meet David, the lawyer, at the Italian Village Restaurant. He welcomes us into a small private room with a table for six. A waiter takes our drink order and leaves us to talk.

"I want to give you a report," David says, and hands each of us a stapled copy. "Then I can try to answer any questions you have."

The room is quiet except for the shuffling of papers and the clanging of dinnerware.

I break the silence. "This doesn't tell us what actually happened. Does Wheaton know what went wrong?"

"When Wheaton staff made statements, they had their lawyer present," David says. "They also hired an outside firm to investigate. So, they should know."

"All those articles," Pat says—I shift in my chair toward her—"remain out there forever."

"The school should do something," Elesha says, "and not make Ethan the scapegoat."

"I spoke to the other boys," David says, "and they were also upset with the press reports, but normally the way this works is I approach the school. If they agree to settle, they normally require a privacy disclosure. If they don't, you file a lawsuit and it becomes public."

"Privacy disclosure? You mean like a gag order?" Johnathan asks.

"The bare minimum we'll need," I quickly add, "is a statement that Ethan's death was not his fault. Why don't you approach the school and see if they're willing to do that?"

"I thought we had agreed as a family," Nathan says, "that we'd talk first. Then we can let David know if we want him to represent us to the school."

Everybody waits, looking over at me.

"We can do that," I say, "but we'll need to quickly go back to the hotel and talk. Johnathan has a flight to catch in a couple of hours."

"Okay," David says, "if you have questions, call me. Let me know what you decide."

In our hotel room at the Homewood Suites, Johnathan stretches out on the king-size bed. Elesha and I sit on the sofa, Pat and Perry across from us in chairs, and Nathan by the window.

"I think we should have David represent us," I say, looking at Pat.

"Dad," Nathan says, "you just spoke at their chapel. I don't understand what we are doing."

"I spoke like they asked me, to bring comfort to the students, and now I'm going to find out what really happened."

"Christians shouldn't go to law against one another!"

"Nathan, I know how you feel," Johnathan says. "I felt the same way until I researched it. When Paul writes that to the Corinthians, he's talking about going to court over trivial matters where you're defrauded of money."

"Obviously, they can never compensate us for the loss of Ethan," I say.

Nathan moves forward in his chair and says, "I see dangers. It could hurt the cause of Christ if we end up in court. We don't want to go down that slippery slope."

"It's not just one thing," Elesha says. "There were several ways it could've been prevented, and now Ethan is the one who is blamed in the papers. It's a lie. It's not right!"

"Let me read a verse," I say, as I get up and take the Gideon Bible out of the hotel drawer. Paging through the Bible, I find Lamentations. "Here it is—Lamentations 3:35–36: 'To turn aside the justice *due* a man, Before the face of the Most High, Or subvert a man in his cause—The Lord does not approve.' Other translations," I add, "such as the English Standard Version, say, 'subvert a man in his lawsuit.'"

"The school," I continue to say, "has positioned us in such a way that we need a lawyer."

"Are you sure," Perry interjects, "they won't deal with us directly?"

"Why not go to them and just try to resolve it without David?" Nathan asks.

Looking around the room, my mind processes that possibility, and I recall Paul's words to the Corinthians, "Have someone in the church mediate."

"Okay! I'm willing to ask President Ryken straight up if we need to hire a lawyer for them to talk to us."

It's a forty-minute drive back to the school. Elesha and I jump in her car, while Johnathan and Nathan are off to the airport in Nathan's car.

At President Ryken's house, his teenage son stands in the driveway bouncing his basketball. He tells me his dad is at Wheaton's soccer game, their second game of the weekend.

At the game, I find him, and we sit on some steps outside the stadium. "I need to talk with you before we leave Chicago. My family and I met with a lawyer today. His investigation shows that the accident was not a matter of Ethan not paying attention."

Ryken doesn't say anything.

"A lawyer told us that the school did an investigation on how the accident happened. My family and I are willing to deal with the school directly, but I think you want us to have a lawyer to resolve this with you."

"Yes, whatever agenda you have. If you have a lawyer, our board would not meet with you unless our legal counsel was present. Lawyers are trained in these matters. This is not a personal matter between us."

"Okay. I wanted to make sure that was your approach. We'll have David contact your lawyer. But lawyers are expensive. We plan to do what is best for our family and Ethan's legacy just like you need to do what you think is best for the school."

We walk to the parking lot. Elesha sees us coming and gets out of her car.

"Your dad and I," Ryken says, "are on the same page."

A couple of days later, back in Cincinnati, I mail hard copies of my research about restitution to Nathan. He represents many Christians who believe we should not go to court against one another, and I want to hear that position. Nathan will articulate its scriptural basis. I phone him, and we have dinner. We end up at his workplace in Clifton.

It's eight p.m. and we're alone in the building. We're in a room with three desks positioned on three walls, and we sit in chairs on wheels with our backs to the desks, opposite one another.

"Nathan, restitution is at the heart of the gospel. Jesus died for us because justice demands payment for offenses against God and others. God calls us to admit our faults and trust in Jesus' atonement. It's a matter of truth and justice."

Nathan is all about the gospel, and I've thought about how I might present my position to him.

"Dad, the gospel calls us to forgive them. You know the parable of the two debtors. The one forgiven much went out and demanded his brother pay him what he owed him."

"Nathan, we do forgive. You can forgive the guy who damages your car, but he must still pay for the damages he caused. If you were injured, he must pay your medical bills and your loss of income from work. Your insurance company would make sure that he does it, even if it means using lawyers. That's why the school has insurance. It's not going to hurt them."

"But Christians going to court," Nathan points out, "is a bad witness to nonbelievers. Our testimony should demonstrate our love and grace. We ought to be able to settle things differently."

"But it is a school, an institution, not an individual."

"They're a Christian school, dad!"

"You know in Zimbabwe as we helped battered women who were married to Christians, we explained to them that forgiveness is not the same thing as reconciliation. Their husband must acknowledge that it is not right for him to beat his wife, and in the name of Jesus, he can't subject her to a life of physical abuse."

"Well, dad, why not just be wronged? This is a one off. Let God judge the matter."

"I am wronged. And it is lifelong. And I'm confronting them to bring about change. I don't want God to judge Wheaton."

"But God doesn't make us pay for our sins!"

"That's because Jesus paid a ransom for our sins."

"Okay, confront them," Nathan says, "and be done with it."

I lean back in my chair, and recall John Stott asking a pointed question in *The Cross of Christ*: Why doesn't God just forgive? Why did Jesus have to die? The simple reason: God's justice must be satisfied. The cross makes no sense apart from the principle of restitution.

"Hey, Nathan, God doesn't remove the consequences of our sins. He forgave David, but David faced the consequences for his adultery and killing Uriah. What a man sows, he reaps! What goes around, comes around."

Our eyes meet.

"Yeah, I understand all that, and I get it that you want to find out what happened, but why should we gain anything from Ethan's death?"

"Parents don't keep track, but they spend countless hours and dollars raising their kids. Money represents time and labor. Not to mention the emotional costs. If you expect reimbursement for damages to your car, the very least a parent should expect . . ."

"But what about people who are martyred for their faith and die in lands where they have no legal recourse or insurance claims? What do you say to them?"

Nathan has a brilliant intellect and could have mastered any subject he set his mind on.

"We share the same hope of the gospel—that we'll see our loved ones in heaven. That is what I tell them. But because others don't have recourse through the law doesn't mean that we don't use what's available to us. They might not have access to medicine or even clean water, but that doesn't mean we don't purify our water or go to a doctor when we need one."

"We need to be different," Nathan says, shaking his head. "You remember my friend? He fell asleep driving. He almost died. The couple in the other car had only minor injuries, but they sued him and his parents for all they could get. Why not just trust God to meet our needs like you always have?"

"I do! And now, I must trust God more than I ever have in the past." *Especially since I don't know why he allowed Ethan's death at such a young age.* "Nathan, I understand what you're saying, but this is a school that charges tuition. They have a responsibility to provide a safe environment. We're not talking minor injuries. We would never want another family to suffer the loss of a child because we did nothing. Something is not right with how this event was conducted!"

"Dad, I love you. You can try to get Wheaton to do something, but I don't want to be a part of it,"

Driving home, I recall what Nathan's friend Tyler once said about him in a note to Pat and me: "It was when I went to your house in Greenbrier that I learned of Nathan's love for his brother Ethan. Now after getting a little older and suffering the loss of my little sister in a horrible winter snow accident, I understand just how special both of your sons were in my life."

Tyler's sister died after her car slid into a snow removal vehicle on the expressway. Right after it happened, Nathan visited Tyler's family. It took courage for Nathan to enter their grief, and he has always had the courage to stand for what he believes.

I don't want to undermine that.

Nathan also has done me a favor. He has helped me examine the issue more closely.

A couple of weeks later, Wheaton's lawyer asks David if we would agree to meet with their trustees and lawyers for mediation. We set a date for after the Christmas holidays.

·20·

Why and How?

"My dad is more upset about my injury than I am."
(FROM ONE OF ETHAN'S SCHOOL PAPERS)

"AT MEDIATION," David says, "a former judge will mediate the meeting between us and the school."

"What about the school making a statement to clear Ethan's name?" I ask.

"They know you want a statement," David says.

"I really need to find out what happened," I add. . . .

Two questions obsess me: why and how did Ethan die?

I know my son was hit by a sixteen-pound weight, but I cannot accept that he died because he was not paying attention. I cannot let go until I find out more. The how question leads me to the why question. What rhyme or reason does his death serve? And I cannot let go of God until I know His purpose in allowing Ethan's death.

How and why—these questions accompany my days like gray skies and rainy days. At times, they roar and hiss like my tinnitus, like static on a radio that is not tuned into a station. My mind is like an airport with bombed-out runways where planes cannot land. They keep radioing the tower amid the commotion, asking for permission to land, longing to arrive. Their fuel runs low, and I hear the passengers scream, "We're dying!"

My mind is crackling and popping like a string of firecrackers!

The why and how of Ethan's death must be connected. They have to intersect like north and south. In life, why and how go everywhere together. Each time I preach, they stand front and center, holding hands for all to see: Why am I here? How am to live? This is why . . . and here is how . . . to glorify God! Why and how lead to one place like two feet walk a well-worn path. But I fail to grasp the way in which why and how are answered in Ethan's death. How does it glorify God?

The relationship between them holds me like a vise in its grip. The why it happened has knocked me down like a huge wave of the sea, and how it happened has carried me out to the middle of the ocean. My thoughts weary me, dog paddling the great deep, longing to grab the unmovable.

But why does it matter?

Answers, even if I had them, would not bring Ethan back to me. The empty longing would remain, looking for his smiling face, waiting to hear his voice call me "baba."

My conversations in Zimbabwe on why and how a person died float through the air. When I was told of a person's death, I often asked, "How did they die?" Nine out of ten times, I was given no cause of death, only an awkward facial expression and a loss for words. Maybe they didn't know the medical reason. Doctors are hard to come by there. Before long, however, I discovered that my African friends heard a radically different question: not how but why did they die?

In the African mindset, why is the big question at death, especially if the deceased did not die at a ripe old age. Death is a spiritual matter. But you do not ask merely anyone the why question. You pay a spirit medium who consults the dead. The ancestral spirit tells you why a particular person has died and what you must do. Ancestors mediate man's relationship, for the Great Chief is distant, and he does not involve himself in such matters.

But God knows the why, and the strangeness of how Ethan died has stunned my senses: "Should Abner die as a fool dies?" (2 Samuel 3:33–34).

The greatest contradiction in how a person lived and how they died is Jesus: a perfect life of love dies the cruelest, most cursed form of death, reserved for the worst of criminals. Never should such a how happen as it did in Jesus's death. But why God allowed it makes it a revelation:

> He *was* wounded for our transgressions, *He was* bruised for our iniquities. . . . All we like sheep have gone astray. We have turned, every one, to his own way; and the LORD has laid on Him the iniquity of us all. . . . And they made His grave with the wicked. . . . He had done no violence, nor *was any* deceit in His mouth. . . . You make His soul an offering for sin. . . . For He shall bear their iniquities. (Isaiah 53:5–11)

The why and how questions were perfectly answered in Jesus' life and death. He even knew beforehand the reason he would die by crucifixion. He would give his life as a ransom for the sins of the world. But I now wonder if the Father and Son differ at times on the how question. Is there within the first two personages of the Triune Godhead a potentially different methodology? My theology tells me that God the Father and God the Son are distinct persons, and they are revealed in the Bible as each having a will, a mind, and emotions.

I hear Jesus say to his Father, "If it be possible let this cup pass from me." In the Garden of Gethsemane, before facing death by crucifixion, Jesus prays those words to the Father three times (Matthew 26:39). The "cup" refers to Jesus' suffering and his anguish of feeling forsaken by his Father as he endured the shame and pain of hanging on the cross. The utter humiliation of it, even the downright wrongness of it. For the Logos, the Divine Word and reason of God, there should be another way. Are not all things possible with God?

Within my own family we have different answers on why and how we should proceed with the school concerning Ethan's death. Although we differ, I would not say that Nathan's perspective is wrong, nor would I censor it or allow it to come between our love. The Bible teaches that even God, at times, struggles within himself on the course of action he takes with his creation:

> How shall I give thee up, Ephraim? how shall I deliver thee, Israel? how shall I make thee as Admah? how shall I set thee as Zeboim? mine heart is turned within me, my repentings are kindled together. (Hosea 11:8, KJV)

> And God saw that the wickedness of man was great in the earth. . . . And it repented the LORD that he had made man on the earth, and it grieved him at his heart. (Genesis 6:5–6, KJV)

> And when the angel stretched out his hand upon Jerusalem to destroy it, the LORD repented him of the evil, and said to the angel that destroyed the people, "It is enough: stay now thine hand." (2 Samuel 24:16, KJV)

At seminary, when I studied these verses and others that speak of God repenting, I dismissed them to uphold God's unchanging nature. Now I wonder what these Scriptures are trying to tell me. Maybe they could help me understand things that seem incompatible with God's goodness and power.

Also, the involvement of good and evil angels in God's administration of his creation, as I discovered in *The Cleansing of the Heavens*, intensifies my query concerning how Ethan died. In many places, Scripture gives us a glimpse into the deep things of God. Like the tip of icebergs are verses such as "Do you not know that we shall judge angels? How much more, things that pertain to this life?" (1 Corinthians 6:3). I believe God's ways, in justice and mercy, will be evident to all moral beings, angelic and human—down to the smallest detail.

Ethan and I were driving down the highway to a family gathering. A misty rain was falling, and visibility was poor. We saw the red flashing lights of the emergency vehicles on the other side of the divide as we passed the scene of an accident. Traffic was backed up bumper to bumper for miles, a line of cars that continued all the way until we got to our exit. It felt ominous.

Michael Huggins, a lifelong friend, called me. A semitruck had stopped in the rain for some reason. Matthew, his son, was coming home from work, and ran into the back of it. He died on the spot, and Michael and Marie had to identify his body at the morgue. I could not believe my ears. When I sat in their lounge, I had no idea the depth of the questions they faced.

Matthew had recently graduated from college. He was exceptionally bright, athletic, and cheerful. He had a crowd of friends who loved him. Many of them attended his funeral. When I stood to speak, a very unusual thought came into my heart, one I had never had before during the many funerals I've done, the thought that Matthew had died in place of someone else. Another individual would have died that night in the same place where the truck had stopped. With that impression, a recent conversation came to my mind with a mother whose grown-up son no longer believed in Jesus. She was distressed about his eternal destiny.

I shared my impression with that church full of mourners in the form of a question: "What if Matthew died in place of someone else, someone who would have left this world for an eternity without God? Someone who would've stood before God condemned because of the selfish life they had lived, but that God was painstakingly loving that person by giving them more time to turn to Him."

I said, "Your life is a vapor like the mist that fell that tragic night Matthew died. Between you and eternity is a thin veil. It can easily be shaken and fall in a moment no matter how robust you are. Perhaps, there are additional reasons God allowed Matthew to die. Maybe, his death would move you today to give your life to Jesus."

Then I asked the question,

> If you were to die today, do you know for sure where you would spend eternity? If God were to ask you today why he should allow you into his heaven, what would your answer be? Would you tell him you deserve heaven because you have lived a good life? Would you make your claim to Paradise based on rules you have kept, rituals you've done, or a certain religion you practiced?
>
> The Bible says there is only one way to the Father. It is through his Son. You must turn from your own way and by faith receive Jesus into your heart. He is standing at the door of your heart right now, patiently knocking. If you open to him, he will come into your life and rescue you from the second death. Yes, a second death awaits those who live however they wish. Oh, they may appear to live well, even die full of years in their sleep. But if they die in unbelief, they will perish forever.
>
> The second death is a lake of fire created for the devil and his angels. But God loves you. He gave his only begotten Son over to death so you would not perish but have everlasting life. Then, like Matthew, when your body dies, you go immediately to be with the Lord. On Judgment Day,

you will enter the fullness of life and enjoy a resurrected, glorified body.

At Matthew's funeral, several young people received Christ.

I know that how we live will determine why we spend eternity where we do. The how and why question surely intersect in eternity. But does that mean we will only grasp the connection between the how and why of life and death from the vantage point of eternity?

Ethan's death has driven me more personally and profoundly into the subject of theodicy. On how divine goodness and providence allow for the existence of evil, and why ultimately redemption is impossible without a ransom being paid.

*　*　*

The mediation meeting comes and goes. It brings me no answers. I am left frustrated, and I look again at my research notes on restitution:

> Our sin necessitated the death of God's Son. Christ made restitution to God for our sins against our Creator, sins of commission and omission. God also requires restitution in our relationships with one another. For example, if I have a flat roof on which people spend time, and I don't construct protective parapets to prevent people from falling off the sides, I'm liable. Scripture says, "He shall make restitution from the best of his own." Restitution is an act of justice. It includes payment for loss of income. When a life is taken, liability is most grave. "He shall give for the redemption of his life whatever is demanded of him" (Genesis 9:5-7, 12:14-20, 20:1-18; Exodus 21:30-34, etc.). Christ did not abolish the law, and he also taught that if a party refuses to take equitable responsibility, the case progresses to a public trial, because offenses

must be justly resolved, or else lawlessness will reign (Matthew 5:17-20, 7:12; 18:15-18; Luke 19:8-10). God ordained governments and judiciaries to protect us. Paul calls believers to a fair resolution without a lawsuit to protect their Christian witness. Paul did, however, resort to Caesar's court when his Jewish brothers wrongfully sought to take his life (Romans 13:1, 1 Corinthians 6:1-8, Acts 25:9).

It seems the only way to arrive at the truth of what happened is to go to court. That would accomplish my main goals: find out what happened, prevent whatever happened from happening to another family, and clear Ethan's name by correcting the news articles that claim inattention was the cause of his death.

·21·

Surrounded by Mountains

....

"Let's not make them pay."

....

MY FAMILY IS OFFERED THE USE OF A DELUXE, three-bedroom cabin in the Smoky Mountains. At a charity fundraiser, a man named John, whom I've never met, won a free week at that cabin, and his secretary, April, who knows me from a church where I've preached in the past, suggested he offer it to me. No one in my family can go, however, and I'm not sure I want to go for a week in the mountains by myself.

But maybe God wants me alone with himself.

There's one week that I have available. I email my dates to the owner, saying, "If it's booked that week, no pressure to accommodate me."

The owner emails right back. "The cabin is all yours that week."

I know what I must do.

Packing the small bag that I packed for Chicago the weekend Ethan died, I know I must write my son a letter. I must tell him what I would have said to him before he died, if I had been given an opportunity to say goodbye.

In the hallway, I gaze at our last family picture, taken in the wooded area of our yard. Ethan, as usual, is positioned in the middle.

He'll be absent from our next picture.

Whenever I think of special family gatherings of the past, now I think, "Aww, that was before Ethan died!" Or, "That was after." My life's journey is now divided between before and after Ethan died. For time is not measured by clocks and calendars, but by defining events and special moments that trigger our deepest feelings of love and loss, of joy and sorrow.

In the kitchen, I pack a box of snacks for my six-hour drive to the Smokies. Out of the cupboard I grab a bag of chips. There's peanut butter and cereal still there that only Ethan ate. I still can't bring myself to throw them out. I take a bottle of flavored water out of the refrigerator next to a half-empty Gatorade bottle that Ethan drank from. I reckon there must be a thousand things in the house that pre-date that horrific day.

If only those items could somehow summon him back.

Walking out to my car, whatever direction I look at our house—front, back, or sides—I'm reminded of him. He helped me move gravel and wood chips, dig ditches for drainage, take trees out, cut the grass—and he did not complain. Pulling out of our driveway, I want to tell Ethan how much I appreciated all his help. Yes, I will write him what's in my heart, and I will ask God to read Ethan my letter.

Through the rolling, green hills of Kentucky, I drive as my mind wanders. . . .

Ethan's departure was so unexpected and abrupt. I've had to take a long look back. Memories of my son flow into my heart, moment by moment, from hills and streams, from faraway lands, in our yard and in every room of our house, during days of sunshine and rain, in baby pictures to fields of play, all through the years as the days went by.

As I ascend steep roads, the engine labors, and I consider the greatest tests Ethan faced in his life. . . .

"Why is everything so hard?" Ethan asked when he was on crutches.

"Hardness builds character," I told him. "You develop character by facing resistance. It's how you exercise your moral muscles."

Now, I need to take my own medicine. It always easier to preach it than live it. But, oh, how I've loved to preach it.

As is often the case, Ethan's greatest tests revolved around what he loved. He was a gifted soccer player, but he also worked at it. His junior year of high school, his team had high hopes of another state championship. With five minutes left in a big game, the opposing team pressed our goal to break a scoreless tie. Ethan stretched his leg further than what's normal and knocked the ball away from the striker. But down he went. He knew immediately that he had torn his ACL. Banging his fist on the ground, he shouted in pain, "It's over." It was awful to watch. His dreams of playing pro soccer seemed destroyed by an injury. After his knee surgery, the spinal block wore off and his pain was intense. I stayed up with him most of the night.

During his pain and disappointment, Ethan chose to love God more. He believed that somehow God would work his injury for good. His teammate Jackson told me, "I assumed Ethan's spot on the team. Most people, after a season-ending injury, me included, would've been angry. Instead, Ethan was positive, and he made it a point to encourage and help me through each game."

A year later, Ethan's love for God was tested again. He had worked hard on his rehab and was ready to play his senior year. His teammates had voted him captain. But because of his injury, he had missed a critical year in the recruitment process: college coaches couldn't watch him play. The coach at Dallas Baptist University, however, saw Ethan's soccer resume, watched his video performances, and wanted him. He provided round-trip airline tickets to Dallas and showed him the campus. Driving home from the airport after Ethan's visit to Dallas, he showed me a text message: a meeting with his high school coach and the athletic director was scheduled for the next day. Ethan had notified his coaches that he would miss a game, so I wondered what was up.

When we met, I was told that Ethan had violated bylaw 7.2.1 of the Ohio High School Athletic Association for team sports. Although he hadn't practiced in Dallas, he had practiced earlier in the season with a school in Florida. His coach said that Ethan had put himself before his team. Before the week was out, Ethan was kicked out of the program. I was livid. I told his coach that Ethan had missed his brother's wedding in California to play two games, and that last year he had injured himself because of how intensely he played for his team.

Ethan surprised me more than the coach. Even though he was a star player, and they were in the hunt for another state championship, he wasn't angry. He went to the games to support his friends. Twice a week, he loaded a seventy-pound, four-foot tall African wood drum into his car. He beat on it and cheered his team on, and never spoke badly to me once about his coach. I was amazed at how he forgave him and moved on.

His teammate Michael said, "It took the most incredible kind of person to show up in the stands. It demonstrated his amazing character." Michael showed me a picture of Ethan reaching over the spectator fence after the team won to advance to the elite eight. The picture shows Ethan giving Michael a hug. "He looks happier than me!" Michael said.

Ethan's teammates loved him. In an earlier game, he took the ball from a kid, and the kid punched him in the back. He walked away, laughing, but his teammates had to be restrained. They wanted to fight the boy. Before another game, Ethan gave a pep talk in the locker room. Everyone was jumping up and down and shouting, "POP, POP, POP!" POP stood for the Pursuit of Perfection.

My Camry descends an incline and picks up speed. Then, it labors as it ascends to the crest of another incline, making its way into the Great Smoky Mountains.

During Ethan's senior year of high school, his knee didn't feel right. Another doctor and another MRI revealed that his graft was nine millimeters too long. Ethan courageously faced another surgery and more grueling months of rehab. He didn't blame the first doctor. He just kept going deeper with God and passed his test with flying colors.

Am I passing or failing my tests?

I've honored the Lord when I've spoken publicly. At the annual Mason alumni game, they had a moment of silence for Ethan, and I made it a point to seek out his coach before the game. I thanked him for the evening and wished him well on his season. I wanted him to know that I didn't hold a grudge against him for putting Ethan off the team his senior year.

Up and down hills I drive, and as the miles go by, my thoughts go faster and further than my car. Then, I turn off the main road and make my way through a forest and up another hill, arriving at a spacious two-story log cabin. The cabin has a lower level with a walk-out and windows on the three sides. Putting my suitcase in a bedroom and a few items in the fridge, I sit on the back porch and stare off into the distance. The forest of evergreens and the long stretches of valleys and mountains seem to go on forever.

"It's been a while, Lord, since we got away, just you and me," I say out loud.

My writing to Ethan brings on weeping, and the lonely mountains seem to amplify the sound of my crying—as if my cry might echo through the valley, as if it might reverberate through eternity, as if Ethan might hear me crying for him, and God might be moved to answer me!

"It's okay, Lord, if you never tell me why. I will still trust you and love you. And I'll accept whatever answer you give me."

Each day I write to Ethan and each day I cry as if I'm trying to drain the oceans.

"Ethan, how I have struggled to let you go, my son. How I've asked God to tell me why he allowed you to be taken from me."

Each night I pray and forgive the school again. I ask God to help me do what's right, and I can't help wondering what Ethan would want me to do with the college. I saw what he did when his car got bumped. "Let's not make them pay," he said. I also saw how he responded to his injury, and how he acted when they kicked him off the soccer team. He just drew closer to God and kept trusting and serving him.

Again, I see that check on my desk from Bank of America—$333.10—the amount of money left in Ethan's account. It came with a letter of condolence. As I held all of Ethan's money, I wept as I remembered Ethan, Elisha, and me laughing and playing cards at that bank in Dallas while we waited to open that account. In a heartbeat, I would give all I own and my very life to have him back again.

Oh, God, I didn't choose for this to happen!

God's silence is like the school's silence. They don't want to talk about how the accident happened, and God doesn't seem to want to talk about why it happened.

"Lord, I know that your promises cannot fail. That it is impossible for you to lie! I know you have often tried to comfort me. But my pain is perpetual. My wound incurable. It refuses to heal! God, are you not the fountain of living water? Have I grieved you that you have become to me like an unreliable stream, whose waters fail? I pour out my heart to you! Will you not answer me? Will you remain silent? If you do remain silent, I will be like those who go down into the pit."

Each day, the question of what to do pulls on my heart, an intense tug-of-war in my soul, back and forth, like a life-and-death struggle, like the sharp blade of a saw cutting my heart from side to side, like my wanting to live and my wanting to die, like my wanting to pursue the school and my being willing to let go, like the hidden plates under the earth colliding and pushing upward, creating the great mountains.

I sleep, wake, and write, leaving the cabin once for groceries. Only my tears break up the hours. Tears and pages pour out of me, and my days in the mountains are coming to an end.

The day before I leave, I see from my window a deer on the slope of a nearby hill. It's the first deer I've seen. He is facing the cabin. He is full grown, muscular, well fed, with a pronounced, symmetrical pair of antlers, which look like velvet. I wonder what kind of deer he is and what he's doing there. He's not feeding. He is looking upward, holding his majestic head in the air, still as a statue, as if he's listening for something.

I'd feed him if he'd let me. I'd stroke his fur. He lingers. I have lettuce in the fridge. But he doesn't need food or anything from me. No, it's as if he was sent to me as a sign, as if the only thing that keeps him there is an expectant waiting, a careful listening for a response on what course of action this Christian man will take.

Then, he turns to go, and my heart flutters. He moves into the woods, out of my sight.

"I gave Ethan to you," I tell God at last. "I'll do what you want me to do."

· 22 ·

My Darkness into Light

....

"Jesus, my God, turns my darkness into light."

....

MY LEGS UP ON OUR SOFA, I sit parallel to the living room windows with my Bible open, but I can't ignore the activity outside: on a tree by our creek, two bushy squirrels jump from branch to branch as if they're playing catch, and another squirrel zigzags toward our house, stopping and standing on his back legs, and grasping something with his front paws. Beyond the squirrel, birds flutter about, and above them, billowing clouds steadily march through the sky, revealing patches of open blue. The morning light entering our living room announces another day, and I look at the passage before me in Psalm 143.

> Hear my prayer, O LORD, Give ear to my supplications! In Your faithfulness answer me, *And* in Your righteousness. . . . For the enemy has persecuted my soul; He has crushed my life to the ground; He has made me dwell in darkness. . . . Therefore my spirit is overwhelmed within me; My heart within me is distressed. . . . Answer me speedily, O

LORD; My spirit fails! Do not hide Your face from me. . . .
Cause me to hear Your loving kindness in the morning,
For in You do I trust; Cause me to know the way in which
I should walk, For I lift up my soul to You. (verses 1–8).

"There was another way, but it would not have worked out as good."

Where'd that come from? The words, "There was another way, but it would not have worked out as good," linger in my mind with an added interjection, "Not as good by far!"

These thoughts came with an impression of how Ethan is very special to God, of how beautiful his life was, of how many people he touched, of how God truly wanted what was best for him, and of how there is much more to come.

Is this the answer to my question, "Wasn't there another way?"

Pat comes into the living room and says, "I've been talking to God this morning and listening. I felt like the Lord told me Ethan is part of his firstfruits."

"Firstfruits?"

"Yes, it was like Ethan was entwined with God like a child cradled on a father's lap, searching his eyes and putting his hands on God's face. But what do you think of firstfruits? Where's that in the New Testament?"

"In Revelation."

"What does it say?" Pat asks, taking a seat on the couch across from me.

Turning to Revelation 14, I read to her: "Then I looked, and behold, a Lamb standing on Mount Zion, and with Him . . . [the] redeemed from *among* men, *being* firstfruits to God and to the Lamb.'"

Two days later, Pat shouts from the basement. "You've got to see what I found!"

Sitting in my office, I expect her to bring me something. Instead, she shouts again, "You won't believe this!" I hear her footsteps rumbling up the stairs, and she's at my office door.

"Come! Right now! Come downstairs! I didn't want to move it. It sent goose bumps up my spine when I saw it. It's in Ethan's box!"

Down the steps I follow her and into her office. She points at a piece of paper sitting in a box. It sits with other papers under it.

"To Ethan: 'Then I looked, and there before me was the Lamb, standing on Mount Zion, and with him 144,000 who had his name and his Father's name written on their foreheads. . . . They were purchased from among men and offered as firstfruits to God and the Lamb. No lie was found in their mouths; they are blameless.' "

It's the exact passage on firstfruits that we read a couple of days ago.

"I think you gave those verses to him," Pat says, "at Christmas time! Years ago!"

Each Christmas, along with presents and money, I would give our four children verses from the Bible. I would always print them out on a piece of paper, read the verses to them, and hand them the slip of paper.

"Why did you give Ethan those verses?" Pat asks.

"I don't know. It must have spoken somehow to me about who Ethan is."

"Well, I remember thinking how strange to give him those verses," Pat says. "I could understand the other verses for the kids, but Ethan's verses didn't make any sense to me."

"I might've given it to him after he had his tattoo because it says, 'they had the Father's name written on them.' "

"No, it was long before that," Pat says, as she sits in her office chair. "I remember Ethan took his gifts and stocking bag full of candy, and later I put this Scripture you gave him in his box with his other papers."

She looks again at the box with his artwork, his rewards, and his certificates as if she can't believe what she has just found. Then she looks at me with a look that says, "What on earth possessed you to give him those verses?"

Leaning against her door, I read it again, shaking my head.

Pat swivels in her chair closer to Ethan's box and says, "God told me, 'Ethan is part of My firstfruits.' Can you believe I found this?"

"Let me try to find that document on my hard drive," and I hurry up the stairs with the slip of paper in my hand.

Plugging in my old hard drive, I search for the document. . . .

Here's the verse I gave Ethan back in 2007, when he was ten: "As Ethan is crazy about soccer, so in the days to come he'll be crazy about ministry. 'They say they serve Christ? But I have served him far more! Have I gone mad to boast like this?'" (2 Corinthians 11:23 [TLB]).

I recall using that verse as I envisaged his desire for God overtaking his desire for soccer.

Here's another one: "To Ethan Aaron—Merry Christmas—2013: Determined and disciplined Secure and safe! / Rising to the top. Never to stop! / All in preparation. Even the perspiration! / For What's in store? Far more! / He's going places. Seeing faces! / And this you can be sure. God has a plan! / He's more than a fan. He's the man! 'And whatever you do or say, do it as a representative of the Lord Jesus, giving thanks through Him to God the Father'" (Colossians 3:17 [TLB]).

I remember that one too. Ethan was so disciplined he watched his diet before his soccer games and wouldn't eat sugar for days, although at times I tempted him with candy on Fridays.

Then I find the Revelation verses that Pat has just discovered among Ethan's things—from a year earlier, in 2012. They're on the same page with the verses I gave to Johnathan, Elesha, and Nathan that year. No poems or comments with the verses that Christmas. I had cut the page into four and given them each the section with their verses. Now I hold the actual piece of paper Pat had found and I had given Ethan five years ago.

Seeing "They have the Father's name written on their forehead," I think of Ethan's "I Am that I Am" tattoo over his heart.

Seeing "They remained virgins," I think I don't believe Ethan ever so much as kissed a girl.

Seeing "They were offered as firstfruits to God and the Lamb," the word "offered" grips me. What might that mean since most translations don't include the word "offered"?

Seeing "No lie was found in their mouths," I don't recall Ethan ever lying to me, but I do recall when we moved from Mason to the countryside, Ethan arrived late at school two days in a row. They asked him why he was late when he was typically on time. He said, "I'm driving further because we moved." He told the truth, but I thought, *Oh boy, they're going to get us now that we've moved out of the school district.* The King James Bible says, "No guile was found in their mouths." I can't recall ever hearing Ethan use a curse word. He would simply say, "Stupid!"

The passage goes on: "They follow the Lamb wherever He goes." I really like that. BibleGateway comments on the verse: "They are those whose hearts have been made as the hearts of little children who have that purity of heart which touched Christ's heart most fondly." Yes, Ethan embodied the precious qualities of a child: trusting, sincere, pure, teachable, reciprocal, vulnerable, adventurous, playful, excitable, meek, and full of wonder. He was becoming an adult, but his heart was still the heart of a child. How Christ must cherish such a heart.

The Lord whispers in my heart, "May I show you a Scripture?" The words come so tenderly as if God feels all my pain and wants me to understand his heart more fully.

"Yes," I answer.

Clearly, the words come, "It's on page 116 of your Bible," and I turn to page 116. It's the book of Exodus chapter 23: The Yearly Feast of Firstfruits.

What are the odds of a page number coming into my mind that's about firstfruits?

The Feast of Firstfruits gathered the best fruit of an early harvest into God's house. It was an offering that led to the final feast, the Great Harvest. Even so, Revelation 14 has the firstfruits offered at the beginning of the chapter and the general harvest of the earth at the end. But it is the idea that Ethan is an offering that gets me thinking again because when an offering was made to God in biblical times, men were not to bring from their flocks what was blind or lame; they were to bring their best, especially when it came to firstfruits. I had used those verses on giving your best to God when it came to collecting things for Zimbabwe, because we had to ship them all the way to Africa. "Please don't give us things if they're broken." God deserves our best: what is beautiful, without spot or wrinkle, what we would most desire to keep for ourselves.

Ethan was all of that and more.

God wants me to see something in his heart that only eternity fully appreciates!

Two weeks later, Pat says to me, "I want to order a book on heaven."

"I have a book on heaven. Let's see if I can find it before you buy one on Amazon."

Searching my four large bookshelves, I find it. Titled *Heaven*, it's a thick book.[3] Sticking out of the top, in the middle, is a marker, where I must have stopped reading. My heart skips a beat. The book marker has a picture of Ethan on it, the sweetest picture of him at ten years old. The marker says, "I smile whenever I think of you."

Oh, my! It is dated 2008 and was made at school the year we returned from Africa.

"Pat," I call out, "you've got to see what I just found!"

I hurry down the steps with the book and the marker.

"Look at this! Ethan's picture, right in the middle of a book on heaven."

"You found this in this book?"

"Yes! I forgot all about this marker. None of my other books have one in them."

"We got just a couple of these," she says.

"God is really going out of his way to talk to us," I say. "He wants us to understand his heart."

Taking the marker and the book, I scan them on my printer and email them to my kids and my siblings, saying, "Look what I found!" To me it's another amazing sign from God.

In the book, author Randy Alcorn says we'll recognize our loved ones in heaven. I've always believed that, because we read in the great "love chapter," 1 Corinthians 13, "We will know even as we are known," and the Bible tells of people recognizing one another in the afterlife.

The next day, I want to read more, but the marker is not inside, and I ask Pat that evening, "Where's the bookmark?"

We look all over the house but neither of us can find it. Where could it have gone? It's too weird. I'm glad I scanned it and Johnathan uploaded it on Facebook. It's like it has vanished into thin air, like it was never there.

A couple of days later, warmer weather has come. I pull the bedspread back from the sheet, and there, gently lying between the sheet and the bedspread, is the bookmark!

Pat or I must have read in bed, and the marker fell out. I look at my boy's smiling face, and I think about when he sat in bed with us and said, "You really are my best friends."

With moist eyes I place his picture bookmark back in the book.

A few days later, I see the marker with the stack of condolence cards and notes that have sat on my office floor for months on end. I hadn't even realized it had fallen out of the book again. But now here it is among the lives he touched. Uncanny that it would come out in these places, and again, I put his picture back in the book titled *Heaven*.

Our recent discoveries are like pieces of a puzzle falling into place, and they remind me of Ethan's saying on Instagram: "Jesus, my God, turns my darkness into light." The words are written in Hebrew and English, and in Ethan's Instagram picture, taken days before he died, he is facing the cross outside St. Peter's Church in downtown Chicago. In light of Ethan's impending death, it was as if this picture of him had been staged.

I think of the words of the prophet Isaiah, quoted in the New Testament: "The people who sat in darkness have seen a great light, And upon those who sat in the region and shadow of death Light has dawned" (Matthew 4:16).

And I know I must hold onto these answers of "why," which God has graciously given us.

· 23 ·

Tell Me of Your Love

....

Jesus, tell me again of Your love that sought me out.
Describe for me the nails I drove through Your hands.

....

IN ETHAN'S ROOM, going through a notepad, I read these words: "Lord, tell me again of Your love." Ethan's handwriting fills the page.
I've not seen this before.

> *Lord, tell me again of Your love.*
> *The love that can't be compared or comprehended.*
> *My God tell me again of Your love.*
> *The love that created me in Your image,*
> *Knowing I would break Your heart.*

Where did Ethan get this? With the notepad in hand, I climb the steps, holding the banister with my other hand, and march into my office. Slumping into my desk chair, I quickly type a line from his notepad into my search engine.

*Jesus, tell me again of Your love that sought
me out.*
*Describe for me the nails I drove through Your
hands.*

Nothing comes up on my PC except webpages with Bible verses.
Nothing close to what I'm reading. . . .

Holy Spirit, tell me again of Your love.
How it raised me from the dead.
*The One that snatched me from the grips of
darkness and placed me in the light.*

Silent tears, unannounced, fall, and my throat tightens—*Ethan wrote
a love letter to God.*

Dad, never let me forget that love.
*Whisper in my ears, speak to the very depths
of my heart,*
Never let me forget Your love, God!

This sea of love into which Ethan plunged is far vaster than I had
imagined. I cannot fathom its depth. My heart burns, catching but a
glimpse of the tender love my son felt. Reading his words again, I see
that Ethan knew more than I had realized—that it was God who pours
his love into his heart. The love of God is a love that we experience
and trust. Knowing that Love is the creature's highest state, the soul's
greatest achievement. In its purest essence, the heart receives God's
redemptive love as its greatest treasure.

It produces a pure love for Jesus, and there's something very special
about a person's first love for Christ. It is sheer sweetness. When we
delight in the Lord, it's easier to do what's hard like going through the
same surgery and rehab twice or washing dishes all day and sleeping
on the floor at night or giving everyone rides to Young Life or talking
to your friend about God for two hours in a parking lot. Such love far

outweighs our human ambitions, our thoughts of all we might achieve and what we might become; everything else finds its meaning and fulfillment in knowing such love. *Is he who is Absolute Love moved to oneness with such a soul?*

Yes, I would reckon that Everlasting Love would wish to immortalize such love!

Does God at times take his children home because his love is made complete in them? Is this the ultimate answer to "why"? Is the reason far deeper than earthly minds can grasp, one that only eternity can fully reveal?

I think of Andy Shaw, the young church planter in Zimbabwe. He wrote a song to the Lord: "Only you for whom this song is sung. Only you I will live for. Only you I will die for." Andy was murdered outside Harare while praying at Cleveland Dam. He had such an incredible potential to do good, and he left a wife and young children.

"Why?" people asked.

"God will not show us why," I said, "to simply satisfy our curiosity. God is not obliged to answer onlookers, only those who warrant an answer like their loved ones. The question of why is between them and God."

After Ethan died, we had dinner with Pastor Gary and Mary Trenum. They shared our loss: years earlier, their beautiful seventeen-year-old daughter, Terri, died a few blocks from their house. She was coming home from volunteering at the church's summer Vacation Bible School, and she was in a car accident. She loved Jesus more than anything.

Tom Church drove the eight-hour roundtrip from Chicago to Cincinnati to talk with me. Tom had listened to my chapel message online. His seventeen-year-old son, Joshua, was found in the locker room after a swimming workout. His heart had stopped beating, though he had no known prior condition. Josh was a lot like Ethan, a young man who loved Jesus, his family, and others.

Julie Duerler sent me a Facebook message. She and her husband, Jeff, pastor a church in Harrison, Ohio. Their sixteen-year-old daughter, Kayla, a young, devout follower of Christ and a stellar person, also died in a tragic accident.

Many young people who love God die in tragic circumstances!

Stephen, an early church deacon, was the first of many martyrs. There have been hundreds of thousands of martyrs since the time of Stephen, and in the Book of Revelation, John revealed that there is a full number who will die as martyrs before the end of time (Revelation 6:11).

No, Ethan, Terri, Joshua, and Kayla were not martyrs; yet, maybe this is also a pattern. Surely, there have been millions of beautiful lives around the globe who have left this world early (Hebrews 11:37–39). Nevertheless, we believe there is a Sovereign God over everything, and his design, splendor, and soul rule over all in both holy justice and tender mercies.

In science, we test our hypotheses by what is called "repeatable observations." This is the first pillar of science, because if the outcome from data is reproduced time and again, a bedrock principle has been discovered. Now, science deals with physical laws, obviously, but what I've observed is moral—or, I should say, spiritual—and is contingent on God's purposeful and redemptive will.

Pat and I watched "Saint John Bosco: Mission to Love." Bosco lived in the eighteenth century and was known as the apostle to youth, helping many get off the streets and teaching them about Jesus. A teenaged boy who loved Jesus deeply was influential in Bosco's community, because of his purity, wisdom, and Christlikeness. When the boy suddenly died, the community was profoundly affected; many lives were transformed. We cried because the boy reminded us of Ethan.

In each case, when a young, devoted life departs this world, God stirs many for eternity. But more than that, he honors their beautiful life in a most extraordinary way.

A person's first love for Jesus is more special to God than anything we could ever accomplish for him. We catch a glimpse of Jesus' desire to immortalize a soul's first love for him. Consider the scene: Lazarus is reclining at a table with Jesus. The atmosphere is warm and tenderhearted. Lazarus loves Jesus; he ought to—for only a week earlier he lay dead, bound in burial cloths, decaying in a closed-off tomb.

A greater love than Lazarus' bursts onto the scene, however. Mary lavishes a full pint of exquisite perfume over Jesus' feet and uses her long, flowing hair to wipe them. The house, which a few days earlier had held the stench of Lazarus' decaying body, is now full of the aroma of the most luxurious perfume. Imagine the depth of love that would lead a person to part with a year's worth of wages to buy such fragrance to then pour on someone's feet.

Mary's humble and shameless act of devotion is questioned and criticized. Conflict enters the scene. Judas calls it a waste because the poor could have used the money. His criticism sounds worthy of consideration. But the contrast could not be more striking: Mary is generous—Judas is greedy. Mary is humble—Judas is proud. Mary is selfless—Judas is narcissistic. Mary kneels in lowly adoration—Judas stands aloof.

Jesus knows the difference.

There is, however, far more to the story than the contrast between Mary and Judas. We must not miss what is most essential. Mary is prompted to break the alabaster box because she knows what Jesus has done for her and what he'll soon do. She has purchased Christ's burial ointment, fit for a king. Jesus is going to die. In contrast to Mary, the disciples are clueless about what will soon happen, and thus, Jesus' death will leave them terribly disillusioned.

Mary expresses her love for Jesus, discerning the scary truth that God will work his greatest miracle in an unthinkable way that is totally countercultural and even scandalous. It is the way of the cross—that terrible stumbling block, that extreme offense, that divine folly. For those who follow Jesus, it is easy to be attracted by a vision of the Christian life that is filled with promise, fellowship, and even demonstrative worship, but has no real understanding or room in it for pain and suffering, crucifixion and death, or denial and dying to self, which is the way of life to which Jesus calls us. These things make no sense—they are foolish to the natural mind, a great waste of human potential.

But wherever the gospel is preached, we see Mary of Bethany immortalized because she willingly broke her alabaster box for Jesus.

That box represents our life—our unique gifts, costly talents, priceless personalities, and God's own image and likeness within us (2 Corinthians 4:7). Breaking our boxes means we willingly give our all to Jesus. Therefore, we lovingly pour out our entire life and soul, all at once or over our many years on earth, as he wills, for his glory, because he is worthy of our all. To many that might seem a waste, especially when a young life with enormous potential for good is taken.

"For we are to God the fragrance of Christ among those who are being saved and among those who are perishing. To the one *we are* the aroma of death *leading* to death, and to the other the aroma of life *leading* to life. And who is sufficient for these things?" (2 Corinthians 2:15–16).

The truth remains: there's nothing better we could ever do than lavish our lives on Jesus. He is more costly than life itself, and our sacrificial love for him will be heralded forever, even as his ultimate sacrifice for us evokes our worship through all ages, world without end.

Too often, we give our Lord only what is left over. Our talents we employ for our own benefit. Our treasures lie elsewhere. But when we realize we have been forgiven much by his dying our death, we will love much, and we will break open our boxes because we know that without him, our lives are meaningless, and our moments, hours, days, weeks, and years amount to nothing apart from our love for him.

The loss of our first love for Jesus is thus the greatest possible tragedy (Revelation 2:4–5). There's no one or anything to which our love can be legitimately transferred. Alas, the loss of our first love for Jesus opens us to every other loss—the joy of our salvation, a sense that all things are new, and a delight in worship, to name but a few.

Love for God is our greatest virtue (1 Corinthians 13:13). Christ is the groom. We are his bride. This is a great mystery (Ephesians 5:23–33). But when we are joined to the Lord, our spirits are truly made one with his Spirit (1 Corinthians 6:17). When we love him, he pours his love into our hearts by the Holy Spirit (Romans 5:5), and only God's love at work within us can motivate us to break open our alabaster boxes.

But we do not like what is broken. We would wish to save ourselves from breaking; yet, we are broken. Jesus personally knows all about our brokenness. He experienced it for us when they stretched his legs and arms out on the cross, and they drove nails though his flesh to hold him there. He poured his soul out unto death for us. He gave us his all. He is the ultimate alabaster box broken to anoint our dead hearts that they may truly live a life of love.

Ethan's prayer has become mine: Jesus, tell me again of your love for me. Describe for me the nails I drove through your hands. O Abba, Father, let me never forget your love!

·24·

You Have Answered Me

....

*"Suffering can be beneficial in ministry
to bring people closer to God
and enable them to minister to others."*

....

AMONG ETHAN'S PAPERS, an essay he wrote on "The Purpose of Suffering" catches my eye. He was studying the big questions like why there is evil if God is all good, and why there is suffering if he is all powerful. "Suffering," Ethan wrote, "can be beneficial in ministry. I intend to prove this by using Bible examples."

My stomach tells me it's time to eat, and I survey yesterday's leftovers in the fridge. Pulling out Tupperware with meatballs, tomato sauce, and penne noodles, I grab a bowl from the cupboard, and set down Ethan's paper on the countertop. Two microwave minutes should do it, and I swing the door shut with a bang.

Picking up Ethan's paper, I see he highlighted the greatest purpose of all in suffering: "Jesus suffered to reconcile us to God!"

Many times, I've read Psalm 22, a prophecy of Jesus' suffering, but it was only after Ethan died that the words "You have answered me" flashed before me like lightning. For twenty-one verses, the psalmist graphically describes his desolation:

> They pierce my hands and my feet. My body is dehydrated. My bones are out of joint. My heart melts within me, and my tongue sticks to the roof of my mouth. I count all my bones. They look and stare at me. They part my clothes among them. You lay me in the dust of death.[4]

Yet, like the psalmist, all my life I have served you, and his heart-wrenching question, "Why then have you forsaken me?" lends itself to a series of questions that hang heavily in the air:

> Good God, why have you allowed wicked men to pierce my hands and my feet? Why do they mock me and hurl their insults, and you do nothing? Why are you so far from helping me, and from the words of my roaring? I cry out to you for answers in the morning, and in the evening I'm not silent, so why don't you answer me?

The microwave beeps, and I set Ethan's paper on a tray, and with a bump I place my bowl of hot pasta next to it. Into my office I go to eat and ponder the purpose of suffering.

Yes, the words "You have answered me" have come alive, and they dance before me. God heard Christ's cry and fully answered him as to why he suffered and died: God will redeem humankind through his suffering, all the ends of the earth will turn to God, multitudes will be saved, even those who have died and those who have not yet been born. "They will come and declare His righteousness to a people who will be born, that He has done *this*" (Psalm 22:22–31).

I slide my lunch tray onto my desk and push other papers on the desk to the side to make room for my pasta.

God gave crystal-clear reasons why the Messiah suffered, and yet at first everybody missed it. The cross blindsided them, even as my son's death blindsided me. The disciples on the Emmaus Road didn't recognize Jesus until he explained God's story to them. Like them, I needed again to hear the story I am a part of, lest I miss the plot: Abraham and Sarah endure the heartache of barrenness before their Isaac is born. "Everything is against me!" Jacob exclaims before he discovers that Joseph still lives. Righteous Job loses his children, his wealth, and his health before God restores double to him. Moses spends forty years in a desert before he delivers Israel out of Egypt. David flees for his life from Saul's javelin before he reigns over Israel as king. It's all one story, and God uses the very things they suffer to bring them to glory.

Ethan wrote, "Joseph suffered to save his family," and it is as if my son wrote this paper for me, as if he sits and eats with me, wanting to tell me our story. Joseph's brothers sold him as a slave. Years later, he told them, "You meant it for evil, but God meant it for good." God used the bad will of Joseph's brothers to bring about his good will. They were responsible for their jealousy and betrayal, and although God hated their lies and discord, he did not intervene. Why? Because he intended to bring good out of it.

Christ sums up our story in the most basic terms possible: "Was it not necessary for the Christ to suffer these things and to enter into His glory?" (Luke 24:26, NASB). Mark, don't forget the plot: suffering before glory, going down before going up, pain before gain, thorns before thrones, crosses before crowns, and death before resurrection. This is his-story and ours. Through the centuries, it repeats itself again and again with equal fury, and I must hear it again and again lest I forget.

Steam rises from my bowl, and I chew the hot pasta gingerly, and slowly take another sip of my fizzy, lemon-flavored water.

I find the ultimate answer to my "Why, God?" question in the good news of Christ, in his suffering and dying, and in his rising and glory at the Father's right hand, in his coming again to redeem his people and restore his creation. It is through God's Son that God speaks to me concerning my son's death and why I have suffered grief. All my answers are found at the cross: *Did the devil instigate Jesus' death?* You bet. *Was it evil?* No greater evil ever perpetrated on earth! *Did God allow it?* Absolutely! *Did he hold Judas, the Sanhedrin, and Pilate responsible?* Certainly! *Did good come out of it?* No greater good possible than the redemption of all who would believe it.

My mind mulls over the fact that all these things also apply to my son's death.

I love pasta. Growing up, my grandma came to our house every Thursday to make us dinner. All afternoon, she cooked a rich spaghetti sauce from scratch and made the best meatballs from chunks of beef. I can still see her at the stove, stirring that big pan of sauce as the aroma fills the kitchen. It was my favorite meal of the week.

Yes, we must get God's story right lest we lose heart when tragedy strikes. God is not punishing us. He's bringing us into deeper communion with himself and bringing others to himself. When we get the story right, we can combat the devil's lies and take courage in our losses. We can identify with Christ: his sacrificial love, his humble heart, his deep empathy, his confident relationship to his Father, his wise means of overcoming evil with good, and every beautiful facet of his nature! As a result, we can experience his higher order of good: faith, hope, and love, which are not possible without free will and obstacles to overcome.

The "why" question is a great obstacle when suffering and death strike. We cannot help desiring answers. I believe what God has shown me concerning Ethan's death applies to many bright lives that depart this world. And I believe it will help us understand his awesome ways in the world, his way of love and faith in Jesus, his mighty redemption through suffering, and our participation in his heroic story of life.

Oh, God you have answered me.

The revelation of God's love in Christ answers life's great challenges. His love working by faith never fails to overcome. Yes, the greatest virtue God imparts to us is love. But we do not often think of love in terms of suffering. Yet they go hand in hand. In defining love, the first thing Scripture says about love is that "love suffers long . . . bears all things . . . endures all things" (1 Corinthians 13:4–7).

My fork captures more noodles, another mouthful of tasty red tomato sauce, slight pepper and herbal flavors, a tinge of sun-dried tomatoes. *Pat can also cook.* I like penne noodles better than the long spaghetti noodles. They are easier for my fork to get hold of and penne noodles hold more sauce—and isn't that the purpose of noodles as they fill your hungry stomach?

In his book *The Problem of Pain*, C. S. Lewis reframed the question of God's role in suffering by saying, "The real problem is not why some pious, humble, believing people suffer, but why some do not."

"The Apostles," Ethan wrote, "suffered to bring the message to others."

God explained to Paul why he suffered. "I now rejoice in my sufferings for you, and fill up in my flesh what is lacking in the afflictions of Christ, for the sake of His body, which is the church" (Colossians 1:24–27).

Paul did not earn his salvation by suffering, nor did he add anything to what Jesus suffered to redeem us (Hebrews 9:26). But his suffering was necessary so that others could hear the message and be saved, and in his suffering, God gave the apostle power he had not known (2 Timothy 2:10; 2 Corinthians 12:6). Christian suffering thus offers us the most glorious answer to suffering ever given humankind, for it is a participation in Jesus' Messianic mission. That's true not only of missionaries who suffer hardships and persecution so that others can hear and believe, but also for all Christians as they suffer rejection for Christ's sake.

Love suffers long, and suffering tests our love for God and others. I reckon it is the most Christlike thing we do for others. That's "what is lacking in the afflictions of Christ."

I finish the last couple of noodles, flakes of parmesan cheese, and a green basil leaf. Only a remnant of sauce remains on the side of my bowl.

In this present evil age, I believe God only permits suffering for a finite time and for a redemptive purpose. He also promises to fully reward us in eternity. Christ's suffering was redemptive, and I believe God intends that our suffering also serves a redemptive purpose both in our lives and in the lives of others. When we suffer, he calls us to trust him.

I believe there is no better world God could create. It allows us the capacity to love freely and to choose to trust God explicitly. Freedom allows pain and evil for a season, but God decided in advance to work all things, even evil and painful things, together for a greater good. We learn more from pain than we do from pleasure, and if God prevented pain regardless of what we did, we would become the most reckless and self-centered people imaginable. Not only do we learn obedience through the things we suffer, but we also learn compassion (Hebrews 5:8).

God not only answered our question of why, but he also gave us answers to other questions, such as, "What is Ethan doing in heaven?" For example, Pat's cousin Jenny, who is battling cancer, emailed us:

> Hi Pat, I fell asleep this afternoon and had quite a dream. I was walking with a large group of young adults, going to a huge event, walking up a long, winding, paved walkway. I began singing a short tune as a song of praise, but I had no words. A young man caught up with us and began putting words to my song, such as "Thank You for this day you

made." It was Ethan. He had a light, a goodness, and a purity to him. He sang louder as we went! Then he became very excited and ran ahead of us in this beautiful park and up a steep incline of some twenty feet. It was then that I knew he was one of the pastors that everyone was coming to hear that day. I woke up after that, as I had to pause before going up the incline. Ethan was full of joy and certainly continuing to follow his dreams.

Pat and I had just read *Within Heaven's Gates*. Rebecca Springer shares this vision of heaven: "We will go to the grand auditorium. Martin Luther is speaking . . . John Wesley. There may also be other speakers. . . . This great auditorium. . . . It stands on a slight hill."[5]

Now I can imagine Ethan full of life and delight, serving Jesus in heaven, and I reckon the Father had him on a fast track to be with him because God is love.

More difficult and pressing questions confront believers; yet the biblical view of suffering—as redemptive—is clear. That answers a big question, and the Holy Spirit shows us specific answers that fit into that framework. These personalized answers, when properly interpreted, will always help us endure and overcome what we suffer. In our suffering, God walks and talks with us.

Pat and I recently traveled to California to see Holly and Johnathan. We checked into the Lighthouse Lodge in Pacific Grove, our first time staying there. We pulled back the curtains leading to a balcony, and surprise, several deer, fifty feet away! I counted twelve of them, and they included young fawns. They were all in an old graveyard, and a buck amazed me, lying on a grave facing a headstone. Moments later, when Johnathan and Holly arrived at the hotel, the deer were still there. Johnathan couldn't get over that buck lying on a grave facing the headstone. Deer in a graveyard outside our hotel room was a first in all our travels.

"God is speaking to us again," I said to Johnathan and Holly. But Pat said it best: "God has had an ongoing conversation with us." Yes, an ongoing conversation. I've needed that.

As he has done for multitudes before us, God speaks redemptive words to us in many unique ways. The slip of paper with the verses from Revelation that I gave Ethan rests in my office as a reminder— God answered us! Even if Pat hadn't heard the word *firstfruits* before we found those verses, we would've still believed Ethan was special to God, because that's what Scripture teaches. The same goes for Ethan's picture on the marker inside the book about heaven. These Spirit-given discoveries, however, encourage us to overcome our loss. God loves us and he is not silent in the face of evil. His soft voice is louder than Satan's railing; his gentle touch is stronger than that steel weight that crushed my spirit.

"You have answered me!"

Speaking of answers, I was in Egypt for a week, outside Cairo, teaching a group of pastors from my book on God's sovereignty, which had been translated into Arabic, when the question arose: "How can an all-powerful, all-loving God allow Herod to kill all those innocent babies in Bethlehem?" An answer came to me in an instant like a download on a PC: "What if, God made it their eternal glory that their infant souls died in place of the Christ child? Nowhere else does anyone die in place of Jesus! What if their weeping parents are consoled forever with joy unspeakable and full of glory, knowing their precious little ones died a premature death meant for Jesus, so that when his time came, God's Son could die upon the cross to take away the sins of the world? What if they escaped the many troubles of this world, and found that it is their enduring honor to have died for Christ like no other group?"

I place my bowl in the dishwasher. My heart is full.

·25·

A Full Circle

....

*"In my understanding, ministry is built on
knowing God, which translates into the way we love him and
the ways we love our neighbor; these then culminate in the
community we build so that we might push
one another to run the race well."*

....

JOHNATHAN AND I are back at Wheaton College. He flew in from San Francisco today, his fourth set of flights to Chicago in the last year. I drove from Cincinnati and picked him up at the airport. As we headed to Wheaton, he read me a tribute he wrote for his brother:

> For us, what happened to Ethan was unthinkable. We were with him from his first cry. We loved and cherished him more than words can express, and we are now determined to honor his life. Ethan lived his life with excellence, integrity, and great honor. His guiding principle was "Living for the One who died for me." It's our responsibility to afford him the same honor he gave to God and others.

Together at Wheaton College we accept the school's offer to make a joint statement to clear Ethan's name, clarifying that the accident was not Ethan's fault. The school will also endow a generous scholarship of over $500,000 in Ethan's memory. The Ethan Roser Memorial Scholarship will benefit two students each year who are studying for Christian ministry, preferably transfer students like Ethan. It is a way that Ethan's legacy will live on at the college.

After our meeting, I say to Johnathan, "I wish we could have done this a year ago."

"I think we had to go through this whole process to get this point," Johnathan replies.

"I was fortunate to find David. He understood our desire, but I think nine out of ten lawyers would've had us in court."

"I really like him, dad. He was a godsend. We had to honor Ethan this way."

"I love the tribute you wrote."

"I know President Ryken was sorry," Johnathan says, "that he gave us the impression that he had reached an early conclusion that the accident was Ethan's fault. He simply wanted to share what limited information he had. They too were asking how it had happened."

"Yes, I know that he didn't intend to say anything that added to our grief. I was obviously hurting, worse than I have ever hurt. They have a lot to deal with running the school. I can see why Ethan loved it here. Wheaton is a special place. God has helped us resolve things in an equitable way."

"Dad, I think they should have an insurance policy in place in case someone gets electrocuted or a railing gives way. God forbid anything like that happens."

"Yeah," I reply with a sigh. "I imagine that would've helped."

"But how are you feeling, dad?" Johnathan asks.

"I feel a heavy weight has been lifted off my shoulders. But a year from now—or five years from now—I'd hate to hear that another family is grieving the loss of their child from a hammer throw. How would I feel if I did nothing to prevent it? Another family asking, 'How did something like this happen?' Why hasn't anybody done anything?"

"The NCAA's protocol for the event is far too loose," Johnathan says. "It leaves way too much up to the schools. That is where the changes need to be made!"

"But Wheaton can't change the NCAA rules. Their statement says they will address the systemic issues within the hammer throw protocol within their conference to make the event safer."

"Something needs to be done for all the schools," Johnathan says.

"Do you think it could happen again?" I ask.

"Well, it's happened before, and it has happened to us."

"Well, now I know more about how it happened. Years ago, the NCAA could've done any number of things to make the hammer throw safer for Ethan. If," I add, taking a deep breath, "they had simply required officials to be certified—had mandated a safer cage, took everyone off the field during warmups, blew a whistle before they throw that sixteen-pound steel weight hundreds of feet in the air, made a notation in a chart before and after each throw, just like they measure each throw, something to make it safer. But they did nothing, despite the recommendations."

"The NCAA needs to do something now!"

"What'd you think about pursuing the NCAA?" I ask.

"Dad, that would be the right thing." Johnathan pats me on the shoulder. "It may take time with the NCAA, but I think we should do it. You know they are changing the rules for football, concussion protocols, targeting, and stuff like helmet to helmet."

"It will be far easier for me emotionally to deal with the NCAA than the school."

Johnathan waits for me to say more—to share my concern—but now I'm thinking of Ethan: how purely he loved, how freely he lived, how untainted by the world.

"Dad, don't worry about what anyone thinks," Johnathan says. "God knows your heart. You've been patient and acted honorably."

I leave Chicago at 8:25 p.m. to head back home. While driving, I decide not to call the *Tribune* or the *Cincinnati Enquirer* to get articles in the paper regarding our joint statement. It will be issued on Wheaton's website only. Instead, I decide to talk to David and ask if we can pursue the NCAA to make the sport safer. That is another way we can honor the beautiful life Ethan lived.

Dr. Ed Stetzer, who holds the Billy Graham Chair of Missions at Wheaton College, wrote an article titled "Being Remembered for What Matters":

> Jerry Root, on our team here at the Billy Graham Center, was Ethan's professor. As he talked with Ethan, it became clear that Ethan had a deep and abiding love for the spread of the gospel. Student after student acknowledged his warm heart. One student remarked that "he yearned for people to know God's love." Story after story . . . he provided our campus community with such a clear picture of what a Christ-honoring, gospel-transformed life really looks like. This is not the first time that our campus community has grieved the loss of one of its own. Perhaps the most famous loss here was the deaths of graduates Nate Saint, Jim Elliot, and Ed McCully in January of 1956. That event on the shores of Ecuador shook the college and the country. If you know the story, their deaths galvanized others to go to the mission field. My hope is that will happen today as well—that students (and faculty and others) will grieve, question, and struggle, as we always

do in moments like this. But that we also might take up the baton with which Ethan ran—and share the Jesus he knew and wanted others to know.[6]

A few days later, our doorbell rings. "They're here," I call to Pat from our foyer.

Michael Besse stands at our door wearing a handsome suit and carrying a beautiful bouquet of flowers, which he gently hands to Pat. He then gives us both a big hug.

Pat has invited a few of Ethan's friends over to share memories of our son, and Michael is the first to arrive. He played soccer with Ethan at Mason, and they've been close friends since middle school. Pat brings a tray of pastries and cookies into the living room.

"I'd love to hear stories about Ethan, secrets and all," I say, as I pass a plate to him.

Michael leans forward on the sofa and says,

During spring break our sophomore year, we were tired of seeing social media posts and pictures of beach vacations. Ethan had an idea. He, Kyle, and I went to Kroger and picked out a lobster. We named him Larry the Lobster. We went to Dylan's house and placed Larry inside their mailbox. By now, it was dark out. I called Dylan, saying, "My mom put a check in your mailbox for soccer. She asked if you got it." We waited, watching from our car down the street. Sure enough, Dylan came out. He reached inside the mailbox and felt Larry and immediately jumped back. Then he peered inside the mailbox with his phone flashlight, which lit up Larry's ugly face and claws. It scared him so bad he stumbled backwards onto the pavement. We laughed so hard we cried. It was one of the funniest moments of my life.

"What a character!" Pat says, taking a seat on a wingback chair.

I had never heard that one before, but Ethan enjoyed playing pranks.

Michael places a pastry on his plate, and I can tell he has fond memories a mile long.

"When Kyle and I told Ethan we would come to Timberwolf," Michael says, "Ethan was so happy he kissed us on our foreheads."

"The kiss on the forehead," I say, "he got from his oldest brother, who would give Ethan a kiss on the forehead when he came into town."

Michael adds, "It was amazing how he volunteered to work in the kitchen at Timberwolf, standing for twelve hours a day. That really impressed me. I mean, he was recovering from knee surgery and needed to do rehab for soccer. Our sophomore year we started going to the GMC Cross Country meets. 'They come to cheer for us,' Ethan said. 'We have to do the same for them.' He made ridiculous signs and screamed more than anyone. The runners weren't used to that. They kept thanking us. We did it for three years. We'd get Chick-fil-A for breakfast and then head over to watch them run. It was my favorite weekend activity. One year, Ethan hobbled around on crutches, still rushing from the starting line so he could cheer for them at the finish line. It was so cool to see his passion for his friends. He touched so many lives. I really believe Ethan was the most positive influence on his peers in our entire graduating class."

It was like a special anointing rested on Ethan the last two years of his life—like in a book I read called *Anointed for Burial*. Before the Khmer Rouge committed genocide in the killing fields, God put a special anointing on the Cambodian church to touch lives. Now there are a thousand times as many Christians in Cambodia, just as I dream of "a thousand-thousand Ethans" one day.

Taylor arrives, and she smiles at me as she enters the living room. "Ethan told me more than once, 'My dad is my best friend!'" she says, as she sits across from me. "I wanted to tell you this story from Frontier camp with Ethan. We climbed to the top of a mountain, to a cross that stood there. We both saw what a little bit of heaven would be like." Taylor's eyes are radiant, and she says, "Ethan cared for me more than most people ever will."

Juan, Ethan's friend from Venezuela, arrives and sits by the window. "We're telling stories about Ethan," I say.

"At camp," Juan quickly says, "Ethan stayed up for hours answering our questions and explaining passages. His energy was absolutely infectious. I got to know your son well because Ethan and I did skits for Young Life."

"Tell us about one of the skits," Pat says, as she passes him the plate of goodies.

> It started with our cue, blaring Mariachi music. Swinging a door wide open, Ethan bolted out in front of me, legs swaying and hair flying. We jumped over kids. When we got to the front of the room, Ethan was bouncing around like the Tasmanian devil, pretending to play on his air guitar. He sang his heart out, matching the Spanish words in the song. It felt like time had slowed down. I could tell in that moment he was where he was meant to be, acting like a fool in front of a hundred kids to make them laugh. And sure enough, kids' faces were filled with every emotion: some laughing, some tomato red with second-hand embarrassment, and some in pure shock. Then the entire room swelled with laughter as we threw out one-liners, completely veering off script because of Ethan's energy.

The doorbell rings and more of Ethan's friends arrive. Our living room fills.

"When Ethan was a baby," Pat says, "we visited America. I held him in my arms while a real estate lady showed me a condo, two condos down from the unit we eventually bought."

"Yeah," I add, "God put us in Mason when we came back from Zimbabwe. It was all farm fields when we were growing up."

"Our first Halloween back," Pat continues, "We were in the condo. Ethan heard about Halloween and asked, 'Can I be the Holy Spirit?' 'I'll need to talk to your dad,' I told him." Pat looks at me and says, "You agreed, and Ethan was so excited. I got him a white ghost outfit at Drug Mart for a dollar. He got a bag full of candy and gave out a hundred gospel tracts."

Ethan's friends laugh.

"Many times, I wondered what I'd be doing when Ethan turned twenty," Pat adds. "I knew that would make me sixty. He helped me count the years."

After they leave, I say to Pat, "It was good to hear their stories."

They help me appreciate the beautiful story God tells through Ethan's life.

· 26 ·

Be Bold and Go All In

....

"Be bold and go all in for God."

....

AT A TABLE IN THE CORNER OF A COFFEE SHOP, I put earbuds in to listen to Ethan speak. His senior year of high school, he was asked to share what Young Life meant to him. This audio on YouTube is his only recorded message.

Ethan's voice: "My parents were missionaries. I always heard about God. You know as young people we might see God in older people like I did in my parents, but it is weird when we don't see him in people our own age."

It has been a year since I last heard his voice, and the deepest part of me is stirred.

Ethan says, "It makes it a lot more real when you can see God in friends, and that is what Young Life is all about."

They had asked Ethan to pass on some advice to the younger students.

"I am still young," Ethan said, "and the only advice I can give you is be bold and go all in for God."

Hitting the pause button, I don't want to miss a word. Every day, I spend my first five hours gathering up Ethan's life. In my longing, that is how I spend time with him. Although I've cried a lot, I record his life for those who will not meet him or hear him speak. It's a way to see him live again, to give him a voice once more. But the pages I write are too few, and my time of writing too brief to tell of him. For he is beyond telling. But tell I must, and the best way to tell of him is in his own words.

"By going all in," Ethan explains, "you are definitely going to be bold. I encourage you not to be afraid. Think about the impact you can have! It far outweighs any possibility of people making fun of you, saying, 'You are a weird kid.'"

Ethan bridged gaps between kids at school. He had friends who were jocks, nerds, partiers, and church goers. His friend Alec told me, "The profound impact Ethan had on people was a gift. He never pushed his faith on others. He was so strong in his beliefs that it never even fazed him that others might think he was different. Maybe that's why everyone loved him. Maybe that's why, after he died, my next thought was that I should go to church."

"When you go all in," Ethan goes on to say, "everything that the world has to offer becomes second, and you don't really worry about how people look at you. We might think, 'Yeah, being popular, being famous, being rich' is it. But impacting somebody's soul for eternity so that they know God's love—that is the highest calling you can ever have!"

My son, you did that, and "going all in" epitomized your life.

"I am going to read," Ethan says, "verses in Revelation. It is kind of weird, some symbolism like a lamb with seven horns and seven eyes."

The Unsealed Book sat next to Ethan's bed, my book on Revelation, and Conner, a friend of Ethan, told me, "Ethan brought up your interest in Revelation. This started an intense conversation in his car about God, heaven, and the end of the world. After two hours, he turned to me and said, 'See, I love talking about this kinda stuff,' as if I needed any further convincing. We might've talked longer, but a security car parked by us so we figured we should leave."

Ethan began reading:

> Then I saw in the right hand of him who sat on the throne a scroll with writing on both sides and sealed with seven seals. And I saw a mighty angel proclaiming in a loud voice, "Who is worthy to break the seals and open the scroll?" But no one in heaven or on earth or under the earth could open the scroll or even look inside it. I wept and wept because no one was found who was worthy to open the scroll or look inside. Then one of the elders said to me, "Do not weep! See, the Lion of the tribe of Judah, the Root of David, has triumphed. He is able to open the scroll."

I am astounded that Ethan chose this passage, because in my book I wrote that this passage tells us that only Jesus is worthy to unveil all that is to come. He alone reveals the destiny of all, each person who will ever live, the length and content of our earthly days, and our heavenly inheritance in the world to come.

> And they sang a new song saying, "You are worthy to take the scroll and to open its seals, because you were slain, and with your blood you purchased for God persons from every tribe and language and people and nation." [7]

I know the Lamb of God has determined my son's destiny, and powerful feelings engulf me. I must make haste for the door. In my car, through tears, I say, "Oh, Lamb of God, you are truly worthy! Worthy to receive Ethan's life as the fruit of your sacrifice." Sensing God's nearness, I passionately pray, "My Father, I'm beginning to understand you better. I see what you're doing in the world through your Holy Child—why it is all about Jesus! He alone is worthy to receive our lives as living sacrifices. Ethan is our precious seed that we buried. We water that seed with our tears. May you use his life to reach a thousand Ethans, who will, in turn, reach another thousand. There is no greater ramification of my son's death than the spread of the good news of your Son!"

In my car, I listen to Ethan read the rest of his chosen passage. " 'You have made them to be a kingdom and priests to serve our God, and they will reign on the earth' " (Revelation 5:1–10). I had read this same passage after Ethan died, and as I got up from the sofa, I felt impressed to look at it again. *You'll see something you're not considering!* And the words "They shall reign on the earth" stood out, because a grief book I read in an effort to help mourners "let go" avowed, "Our loved ones will never return to the earth." But the Bible says, "They will return with Jesus and reign on the New Earth forever in a resurrected body." Answers to why God permits evil are inadequate without an understanding of the end of the world, the final judgment, and the meek inheriting the earth. God will remove from creation all that offends, but when the devil and his angels are thrown into the lake of fire, God must doom all who have followed Satan's rebellion. Therefore, God's ways in this world are ultimately vindicated by rewarding the faithful and punishing evildoers. "He will wipe every tear from their eyes. There will be no more death or mourning or crying or pain, for the old order of things has passed away" (Revelation 21:4 NIV).

In the meantime, as he chooses, God redeems our lives and shapes us for eternity. Ethan shared the essence of his life when he spoke that day—his life's message! He offered himself up to Jesus with pure love, and the Father received him for all eternity. He loved his friends deeply, and he had an everlasting impact on them. He could do no better than what God chose to do through his life on earth. He now serves the Lord in heaven and shares in Christ's eternal glory. He goes with the

Lamb wherever the Lamb goes! And I recall after Ethan's memorial service, before we buried his body, saying aloud to God,

"Ethan was so alive."

And softly, I heard the words in my heart, "He is more alive now."

"But Ethan was so beautiful," I protested.

"He is more beautiful now."

✳ ✳ ✳

Reaching our lane, I pull next to our mailbox.

Only God can heal our shattered hearts.

My phone buzzes: a text from Josh who played soccer with Ethan at Wheaton College.

"This Fall I will coach three boys' teams in soccer, and it will be another opportunity to share Ethan's story."

Billy had recently texted Pat: "My life has been crazy since those days at DBU. I am currently teaching and coaching soccer in high school. More importantly though, over a long period of time, I came to realize who Jesus truly is and I am pursuing a personal, intimate relationship with the Father. I want you to know that Ethan played a major role in that, and I am so incredibly thankful for his constant leaning into me as a friend while he was in Dallas."

As I collect the mail out of our mailbox, a lopsided stack of envelopes fills my hands. A thank you size envelope slips out of my hand and floats to the ground.

Who might this be . . .?

"I've worn the bracelet, 'Be bold and go all in,' for three years now since Ethan died." I read Alek's handwritten note. "It has inspired me to love people and seize every opportunity!"

Unlike Josh and Billy, Alek didn't know Ethan well. Yet, Ethan's life has made a huge impact on him.

A thousand, thousand Ethans.

Who will they be? Where will they come from? How will God reach them?

Only God can do that. Only he can take our broken lives and feed others, just as Jesus fed the multitude in the wilderness with a boy's handful of loaves and fishes. But miracles of multiplication start with small things that God enables each of us to do. I think of what Jeremiah told me. He was Ethan's study partner and Young Life co-leader, and he now ministers full-time with YL at Glenbard West High School.

> Ethan and I both grew up in Young Life areas that had Bible studies known as Campaigners. But I was too intimidated as a new leader and a first-year college student to attempt to start something like this on my own. That, however, wouldn't last long because Ethan felt differently about this. After he had transferred to Wheaton and was placed in the same area where I was a leader, our friendship in Christ became what Ethan called, "a new superhero partnership." Soon Ethan radically changed my approach to doing ministry. He was shocked to hear we didn't have a Campaigners group, and he said, "J, let's start one." That was Ethan. Someone who just did things. He was confident. Not in who he was, but in the One whom he knew was inside of him. My thought was, No way! That's going to be too much work for us to handle, and I don't know where to begin. But all that came out of my mouth was "Um, yeah sure but." I won't lie and say he had some fiery passionate far off look in his eyes or that he gave me a great motivational speech. No. He just stood there and grinned at me. His confidence in God rubbed off on me, and I nervously called one of the moms of a student in our area and told her about our idea. She quickly offered us a place to lead our first Campaigners meeting.

Ethan demonstrated a bold, humble reliance on God. "Yeah, you can't do it, neither can I. Only Jesus can!" Ethan told me. Realizing I could not do it in my own power but only submit what I could do to God, silenced my fears. But it was not easy. We started with nine students. That was the most we would see for the next month. The last meeting that we led together had five kids. We were all over the place in our discussion. I thought we had just confused them, and that not one of these kids would want to come back again. Things seemed to go the exact opposite way of how Ethan and I had hoped and prayed they would go.

The Monday after Ethan passed, a young girl stood up in the group. She said how that past Wednesday had meant so much to her, and how things Ethan had said that night really hit home for her. Our failure? God was at work when it seemed like he wasn't. The way the Lord moved that night after she spoke was one of the most encouraging things I've ever witnessed in my short course of ministry. I sat teary-eyed in awe of God. Somehow, without knowing what I would say, I led us through a discussion that had people opening up, left and right. Somehow, a guy showed up, played a guitar, and led us in the most amazing worship. Somehow, we had five times the number of people. And somehow, since then, our Campaigners meetings have looked like Ethan and I once imagined: people who meet, talk about their lives, and look to Jesus. And somehow, God loves us enough to show up every time.

Since then, I have seen what God can do. Young lives let me know how much they love our time together because for once they do not feel talked at. For many kids, it is the first time they are ever asked about their own thoughts, or ever listened to about what they're struggling with. They have found that Jesus understands and loves them right where they are at. That he is what they've been looking for. That he is the only one who can fill the hole inside of them.

Other friends of Ethan also minister full time now with Young Life, like the two Ks: Katie in Columbus, Ohio, and Katy in Lincoln, Nebraska. They too are seeing young lives transformed.

Also, I think of Jake, Conner, Susan, Bob, Charlotte, Bryce, Sydney, Audrey, Nicole, David, Sonika, Brady, Lizzy, Brent, Grant, Rose, Andrew, Jesse, Kyong, Paul, Alice, Isaac, Ryan, Caleb, Seth, Michael, Maggie, Taryn, Larson, Nicole, Isaac, and others, as on and on it goes.

Jesus' miracle of multiplication amazes his followers. So little for so many, they had thought. But little did they know of the One who was at work among them.

Forgive me, God, for not thanking you more for the lives you have touched through my son. Forgive me for when I have scorned the little that I see. When I have not looked to you and blessed what you have given me. When I have not trusted you for what you alone can do.

Inside, I find Pat busy in the kitchen. The smell of tomato soup and steam from a stir fry fill the air. On top of the other gas burner, a rattling pot. My wife is cooking away. Inside the stove, I see a surprise awaits me in a white ceramic dish. I'm getting hungry.

"I haven't told you," Pat says, "what happened yesterday. I was at Walgreen's printing our last photos of Ethan. It was a tender moment, considering I will never print photos of him again—these were our last of him. I wanted to be alone, but I couldn't figure the machine out. The young lady who came to help me looked intently as each photo came up on the screen. 'That is my son,' I said. 'I went to Mason with Ethan,' she replied. 'Everyone knew Ethan. He was the most positive person I knew.'"

"Wow, we'll never know how many lives Ethan will touch."

"Yes," Pat says, "When I see his fingerprints still on the wall above the door frame, you know his teenage ritual of an imaginary slam-dunk and his audible thrilling, roar of victory, I think, *He's in heaven; yet, his fingerprints are still here!* Outside the store in the parking lot, I looked up into the white clouds and sparkling sky and considered the glory of our son's life, how he shined like the sunlit morning, and I felt: *It was meant to be this way.*

In my mind's eye, I see him playing soccer, passing the ball to a teammate, spinning around the opposition, and making a forward pass. He bounds across the field with a steady rhythm in his legs and hips like a wheel turning. His entire body yields to the next play, leaning forward, and rounding his torso, he makes a header into the net. The team explodes, "Way to go, Ethan!" It's a glorious moment. *Glory!* That is it. Ethan exhibited God's glory.

Yes, every life is intended to exhibit a facet of God's glory.

Pat's voice is steady: "For years, wrong beliefs had gripped my mind and plagued my emotions, even though I read the Bible every day. But for eleven years now, I've meditated on God's promises so that my emotions would line up with the truth. What we believe about life drives our thoughts and actions. I sent Ethan many text messages on God's promises, endeavoring to impress on him that life has its struggles, but hardships and pain all serve a purpose, because through them God promises to give us a better character, to give us a spirit of perseverance and to make us more like him. I told him to keep trying, and he knew the grace of 'try, try again.' I also taught him, emphatically, that God answers prayer. When he had a problem, we would stop right then, talk to God, and expect an answer. I had instilled in him an expectation for the best."

"Pat," I reply, "he had, I believe, the very best life imaginable!"

· 27 ·

My Letter to Ethan

....

"God, the only non-contingent Being,
has lived in community since before time.
If we are going to do ministry well, then we must understand
as beings created in God's image,
it is essential for us to live in a Christ centered community."

....

IN SECTION SEVENTEEN AT SAINT JOSEPH'S CEMETERY, I walk gingerly through the grass, between rows of gravestones, and there's Ethan's grave and the granite marker we had made for him: "Ethan Aaron Roser. Beloved Son and Brother. You Turn My Darkness into Light."

The grass has grown lush, and I bend to open the bronze case that holds his picture. Ethan's smiling face greets me. It's difficult to imagine that his body lies a few feet beneath me. I unfold my letter to him that I wrote while in the mountains.

"Lord, please read my letter to Ethan."

My Beloved Son,

When you were a baby, I lifted you in the air above my head and read to you in bed. On my fortieth birthday, you sat on my lap, not yet two, and touched my nose, playing with those funny, toy-mustache glasses I wore. We laughed and played, invented Hall Ball. With you, I relived the joys of my childhood. You brought me so much joy. You were my steady, peaceful stream, carrying me along through my middle years. The few times you were upset, you felt safe to tell me what was in your heart. You honored me that way.

I watched you learn and put into practice the very best of what you saw and heard. Your zest for life was exceptional. You energized everyone around you. You followed Jesus with the same passion that took me to Africa. You had the full skillset for a great minister. I anticipated you propelling me forward in my old age. You would've taken our mission further and faster than I ever did. Always generous, I saw you put half of your pay in the offering. You know I sent your clothes and shoes to Africa. I knew you would like that!

My Ethan, I've stared at your pictures, watched your videos, and read all that you wrote. I've cherished each moment we shared and pondered every memory my heart can resurrect. Now I know myself better: that I've prized you more than life itself. Your feelings and thoughts always mattered to me. You were significant to me in every way. Your dreams became my dreams. Still, I dream of you. In my dreams, you don't know anything has happened to hurt you. I kiss your head where that hammer hit you. I refuse to leave your side for fear that you'll be taken from me. How could I wake up and you be gone?

Your mom cried again this morning when I showed her what you wrote: "It doesn't matter who you are, how old you are, where you're from or the color of your skin. You were brought into this world by your mother. There's nothing you can do to repay her for that."

Mom was so strong those first days. The Wards held a vigil for you. In their living room, I was met by dozens of pictures. They hung at eye level from strings attached to balloons that had floated to the ceiling: pictures of you kicking a soccer ball, in their pool with Adam, at a high school dance. That evening, several kids told me told how you gave them rides to Young Life. How quietly and lovingly you went about touching lives.

You taught me better than I taught you. You showed me that loving and being loved is better than anything we could ever accomplish, any treasure we could possess, or power we could display, or mystery we could fathom. To love and be loved is to truly live!

You lived the truth of community that you wrote about: "God, the only non-contingent Being, has lived in community (Father, Son, and Holy Spirit) since before time."

You had a special way of bringing out the best in me and balancing our family. You enjoyed community with your friends, and you loved them with action. You wanted them to live in community with God's family. Up until the end, you gave yourself to them, and your death has helped bring them to Christ. I'm sure you've heard the great rejoicing in heaven over each one of them that has returned to God our Father.

How the Father must love us and grieve being separated from his children.

On Father's Day, I didn't have the heart to tell your siblings that all I wanted to do was visit your grave. Before I had children, I didn't know I could love so much, and before you died, I didn't know I could hurt so badly. The year Johnathan was born I graduated from Bible college, and graduates were asked to share their favorite verse. I knew mine: "For the Father loves the Son and shows him all he does" (John 5:20). My love for Johnathan was as deep as the ocean. When your sister, Elesha, was born, I wondered, Will I love her as much as Johnathan? Soon she also claimed my heart. When Nathan and you were born, the question of whether I could love you the same as Johnathan and Elesha never crossed my mind. I had discovered that my heart didn't need to divide its love, as it would simply grow bigger. You had such a big heart for people. How infinitely big our Father's heart must be—to love billions of us and to keep track of all the hairs on our heads.

What must it be like to have only one son and to have him die? How great God's love must be for us to deliver up his only son. For a year, I've reflected on how God feels about his own Son's death. Why it is all about Jesus! Why his claims are exclusive. Why there is no other name by which we can be saved. No other way we can come to the Father. Why on the last day every knee will bow, and tongue confess that he is Lord. I get it! Not simply on a rational level but in an intensely emotional way.

Our Father loved his Son from all eternity, the endless eons past, before the worlds were formed. They had lived in sweet, unbroken fellowship. There was never a time when they did not exist together as one—except that terrible time on the cross when Jesus felt forsaken, bearing the curse of our sins. In his humanity, Jesus' soul felt cut off from the Father's love. His heart broke. Such great anguish couldn't fit in a human body. Jesus' brokenness made windows straight into his soul, windows through which his soul was poured out and windows through which his soul is made known to us. Someone defined intimacy as "in-to me see." To see into Jesus' soul, to feel his heart break for love, will break the hardness of our hearts.

Your brother Johnathan posted a poem by Edward Shillito, the English pastor who survived the horrors of World War I: "The other gods were strong; but Thou wast weak; / They rode, but Thou didst stumble to a throne; / But to our wounds only God's wounds can speak, / And not a god has wounds, but Thou alone."

That poem, "Jesus of the Scars," tells us that only a Savior with a broken heart can heal our broken hearts. My son, the day you died, my heart was shattered into a thousand pieces. Although you spoke of dying, and God gave me a premonition of your leaving me for eternity, I didn't understand it.

I was blindsided!

At the Last Supper, Jesus said, "This is my body broken for you," and he told his followers that he would die, but they could not contemplate life without him. Only afterward did his words register. I reckon that God shows us some things, not because we have power to prevent them, but so we can look back and trust him no matter what. God wanted to soften the blow, and he doesn't want us to live in anxiety beforehand.

How many things you must know now, and how many things you wrote that touch me. You wrote, "When we talk on Jesus' cross, if it doesn't leave people in awe, then we aren't doing it correctly. Think about it; everything that has ever happened in the history of the world pales in comparison to what happened at the cross. No statements made on paper can capture the magnificence of the cross. And if at least one person doesn't feel tears well up in their eyes after our talk about Jesus' death, then we are doing something wrong."

Because of you, I cry more when I preach.

When I dropped you off at the airport, not long ago, we hugged goodbye, and I reminded you that you were four weeks old when you first flew from America to Africa. "No wonder I like airports," you said, "and all the people and places!" Your life was an adventure, but little did I know that you would soon depart this old world— that you, our last born, would be first to fly beyond the stars! God had you on a fast track to himself. He can do that with those whom he wills. But oh, how I have struggled to let you go.

When you considered transferring to Wheaton, you texted Michael Besse. ":)Yeah, God has a plan and I'm excited to see how it works out." Many times, I've read your email to Coach Jake: "None of us can truly understand the complexity of what God is doing in our lives, although sometimes I think we all wish we could take a quick glance at his cheat sheet." Did you ask God to show me his cheat sheet? Is that why mom found those verses I gave you at Christmas and I found your picture in the book on heaven? In life, you passed your tests, but I don't know that I could pass mine without God showing me why you were taken from me.

Silver cars driving down the road near our home still catch my attention. I turn to see who's driving, imagining you behind the wheel, heading for our house like old times. It took me months before I could sell your car. The buyer arrived alone, and I asked him how he planned to take it away. He simply pointed to a tow-dolly on the road up the street, and I watched him strap your car down. I wept as he hauled it out of my sight.

Mail still comes to the house for you. We thought we might sell the place because we missed you so much. Memories of you there with us overwhelmed us. Never will I forget one afternoon when I felt an immense void in my heart you once filled, and I stretched across the bed to sleep my sorrow away. Semi-asleep, I sensed a presence over me. In my heart, I heard you say, "Live Baba, live!"

In Hawaii, they say, "Aloha." It means both "goodbye" and "hello." It expresses constant care and affection, which remains through all our hellos and goodbyes. No, I still can't say goodbye to you, and at first, I thought today that I would say, Au revoir —until we meet again. But that was also too final. So, I'll just say, Aloha!

From your grave, I look up into the clouds overhead and wonder if you can see me. Did you see the Livestream of your memorial service? It seemed like the whole Mason community came out to say aloha. Thousands of people around the world were also deeply touched watching the Livestream. I believe in the harvest of souls because of the life you lived, because you were bold and went all in.

Now you have met my dad, and you are again with your mom's dad. You recall when we visited him in the hospital, mom said to you and your siblings, "You can rub his head." The doctors had removed an ugly tumor from his chin, and they patched a large area of his face with a skin graft from his thigh. The pale white skin graft didn't match the skin on grandpa's face, and with big black stitches he looked alarming. But that didn't deter you. You gently stroked his head with your hand, for you knew how to live and love in community. Oh, my Ethan, how I look forward to living with you again in community. But what will I say to you when I see you? I've heard they don't cry in heaven, so I guess I'll laugh hysterically. And how I long to hear you laugh again. Didn't Christ say, "Blessed are you who cry now because you will laugh with joy"?

May our Father read you my letter, and I hope you like the book I've written. My words are not enough. Yet there are tears for you, which will always flow as they do today upon your grave. I will always yearn for you. You are utterly irreplaceable. My love for you is as unrelenting as your grave. I know you cannot come back to me, but I will come to you. Until that day, may God help me to seize each opportunity he gives me. May my loss of your presence beckon me to ask, "What's important?" May it call me to not take for granted what I've been given. I thank God that he gave you to me for the days of your earthly life.

May our Father in heaven tell you that I am ever pleased with you! You could not have done better than the beautiful life you lived. You're among the finest people I've ever known. This morning, I thanked our Father that you are with the Lamb of God. I am comforted to know that wherever he goes you go with him. And I'm grateful my grief is not complicated by regrets of how I loved you. You know I love you, my beautiful one! For I reckon we have loved as deeply as any father and son.

Please save me a seat near you at the banquet table. We will need eternity to catch up for the time we lost on earth!

EPILOGUE

....

*"The final chapter, The Adequacy of God, was my favorite.
In* Knowing God, *Packer deals with Romans chapter eight."*

....

ON AUGUST 25, 2018, our first grandchild was born, a new life, a little girl to cherish. Soon after Perry, Nathan's wife, gave birth to Everly Ruth Roser, we were in the delivery room. Perry looked calm, but Nathan had a wild look in his eyes. I asked him how it went.

"It was pretty rough," he said, "until they gave us an epidural."

"Us?" I asked. "Who did they give the epidural to first? You or Perry?"

Their Great Dane, Django, is full-grown, 120 pounds of dog, and waist-high to an adult. But he knows that Everly, small as she is, outranks him, big-time. But Django doesn't mind. I just got a video of him licking her head when she took her first steps.

Nathan and Perry are happy new parents. In their living room, pictures of Ethan occupy the most prominent place along with his saying, "Jesus, my God, turns my darkness into light." Nathan ministers to college students at the University of Cincinnati. The impact Nathan had on his little brother's upbringing and faith is being replicated in many young lives. Yes, God is using Nathan to reach "a thousand-thousand Ethans."

Johnathan ministers in San Francisco, and Holly owns a fitness studio. They call us regularly. Johnathan loves to talk about his little brother. Pat and I make mission trips, speak at churches, and do conferences. Ethan's jar of peanut butter remains in our cupboard, but the gloom is gone. It doesn't fit with what God has shown us. Elesha has a great career at Proctor and Gamble, supports Nathan in his Young Life ministry, and liaises with Wheaton College on Ethan's scholarship. Elesha shares this story I've written about her little brother with the theology scholarship recipients at the school.

In March 2019, after our lawyer approached the NCAA and they refused to accept any responsibility in Ethan's death, we filed a wrongful death complaint against the NCAA. We now await the outcome and are hopeful that the event will be made safer.

POSTSCRIPT
Thirty Points of Comfort

....

"The more I rely on Him, the more I know Him!"

....

YOU MAY HAVE LOST A BELOVED PARENT, grandparent, friend, sibling, or child. You may feel overwhelmed by sorrow because of a broken relationship or the death of your dream. Whatever loss you have experienced, having a time each day to comfort your soul will facilitate healing just as daily exercise strengthens your body.

As I have reflected on my grief journey, I've found thirty points of comfort I'd like to share with you. Below, I list each point, relate an anecdote not previously shared, cite an applicable verse, identify an act of comfort, and provide Scripture readings for either a day, a week, or a month, at a chapter a day.

You can read straight through these thirty points of comfort and then go back each morning or evening to focus on a specific point. You can devote a day to each point, or a week, or a month—equaling thirty days, or thirty weeks (six months), or thirty months (two and a half years). It only takes fifteen minutes a day. For monthlong daily use of each point of comfort, you'll read thirty relevant Bible chapters each month, and in thirty months, you will have read the whole Bible. If you choose to do the monthlong daily readings, use a Bible you can highlight. That way you can accent the verses that speak to your heart. You can also share these points of comfort with someone you care about who is hurting.

1. Tell God how you feel.

"I want my son back," I cried out to God as I lay on the floor in Ethan's bedroom. I was overwhelmed by my longing for my son's presence, yet I knew he would never be coming home again. That evening, Johnathan phoned. "Dad," he said, "I had a really weird dream. I was with Ethan at a hospital. He was in a coma, and I was praying, 'God, bring him back!' He opened his right eye but not his left. I put my hand on his head and kept praying in agony. That one eye looked at me like my praying was unsettling to him. All day that dream bothered me. I concluded that having Ethan back would be like him losing half of his senses. He would have far less of a life than he now enjoys in heaven."

At times, I felt a distance toward God. Then, I would be suddenly surprised by a sense of his nearness. I now understand that he wanted me to come to him with my hurt like all parents who want to comfort their children. God can handle your intense emotions and hard questions. Be honest with him. Pour out your heart to him. David did. So did Job and a host of other people in the Bible.

> "My bones are troubled. My soul also is greatly troubled; but You, O Lord—how long? . . . I am weary with my groaning; all night I make my bed swim; I drench my couch with my tears. My eye wastes away because of grief." (Psalm 6:2–7)

God may not always give you answers this side of heaven, but he will always comfort you. He will let you know in unique ways that he is there for you. In eternity, everything will be as clear as the noonday sun. Until then, he will give you peace that surpasses your ability to understand.

To Do: Tell God just how you feel.

To Read: DAY–Psalm 6; WEEK–Psalm 6, Job 1–6;
MONTH–Psalm 6, Job 1–29

2. Ask, look, and listen.

Because I felt that God was going to do whatever he was going do, I didn't ask him for much initially. However, God wanted me to know that he heard my cry and that prayer matters. Prayer makes a difference inside our hearts; prayer can change circumstances. So, Pat and I began to pray together every morning, and we saw amazing answers to our prayers. After you pray, watch how the Lord responds.

> "Praying always with all prayer and supplication in the Spirit, being watchful to this end with all perseverance and supplication for all the saints." (Ephesians 6:18)

To Do: Pray and be observant—look for God's personal touch.

To Read: DAY–Ephesians 6; WEEK–Ephesians 1–6, Philemon; MONTH–Psalm 127, Job 29–42, Psalm 1–15

Thirty

3. Sleep more.

The morning after Ethan died, we drove to Chicago to get his body. Checking in at the Hyatt Regency in Lisle, Illinois, I was the only person at reception. While the receptionist, a woman in her thirties, processed my credit card, I said to myself, "If she asks me how I'm doing, I'm going to tell her about Ethan. Otherwise, I will not say anything."

Handing me two plastic room keys, she asked, "How are you doing?"

"It's been a real hard twenty hours. My son died yesterday in an accident at Wheaton College."

"Oh, my God, that was your son? That's terrible! I am so sorry. We saw it on the news."

She walked out from behind the counter and gave me a hug. "If there is any way we can help," she said, "please let us know."

I barely got the words "Thank you" out. I was as frazzled and fragile as a windblown leaf. My family had loaded our bags onto a luggage cart and pushed it into an elevator. As I squeezed inside, a mirror revealed unkempt gray hair; a worn, unshaven face; and dark rings around blood-shot eyes. No wonder she had asked me how I was doing. My body was kaput, but my mind was a hornets' nest.

"When he rose from prayer and went back to the disciples, he found them asleep, exhausted from sorrow." (Luke 22:45, NIV)

God, in his mercy, made your body to sleep. Sleep does more than revive your strength; it helps you process what your conscious mind finds too difficult to address or unravel. Not only sleep more, take care of yourself.

To Do: Take a nap, go to bed early, or sleep in.

To Read: DAY–Psalm 127; WEEK–Psalm 127, Job 7–12;
MONTH–Psalms 16–44, 127

4. Say "NO" to bitterness and resentment.

After checking into that hotel and enduring hours of meetings, I still could not sleep that night. So, I went down to the hotel lobby. A heavyset man in his seventies appeared. He wore a patterned charcoal-colored suit, a pink ruffled shirt, and a protruding black bow tie. *Where is he going dressed like that at this time of night?* I wondered. He approached me with an inquisitive face.

"Do you mind if I join you? I'm Steven," he said, easing himself into a black leather chair. "The only funeral I plan to attend is my own." Then he got louder. "For whom the bell tolls."

What a strange thing to say. He must have heard about Ethan.

"You heard about my son?"

"No, what about your son?"

"My son died yesterday in an accident at Wheaton College."

"My condolences," he said. "So, we both hate Wheaton!" And he smiled.

"No, I don't hate them!"

"I'm not a very nice man," he added. "My friends will tell you that. But they're my friends because I own properties around the world, and they enjoy staying in luxury." He then grinned and asked, "Are you married?"

"Yes, for thirty-six years."

"Oh, I do feel sorry for you!"

"I have a beautiful wife. Sounds like you're hurt." I leaned forward. "Christ can heal you!"

"Hurt isn't the word. And yes, I've read the Bible—started reading when I was three. Since childhood, I only slept four hours a night. I am from a family of ministers. But they haven't won me yet. People like me keep preachers in business. I plan to keep it that way."

"Only God can bring a person to real faith," and I looked away from him to check the time on my mobile phone. "It's nice to meet you," I said as I stood.

"Don't lie," he responded.

"Well, I haven't slept much in two days."

"Well, then go and get some sleep. I've slept my four hours," he said.

I will never forget that feeling of strangeness. It accompanied me into the elevator, a strangeness only surpassed by the strangeness of the past thirty-six hours. I felt like I had met the devil.

> "See to it that no one falls short of the grace of God and that no bitter root grows up to cause trouble and defile many." (Hebrews 12:15, NIV)

Hatred, bitterness, and resentment bring no comfort; they will make you miserable (Ephesians 4:31). Avoid bitter people who spread bitterness. Use opportunities with such people to honor God, but don't try to save them. Only God can.

To Do: Choose to forgive and let go of all bitterness.

To Read: DAY-Hebrews 12; WEEK-Hebrews 12, Psalm 1–6;

MONTH-Micah 1–7, Nahum 1–3, Psalms 45–64

5. Control your mind.

The second night after Ethan died, again, deprived of sleep, I had to stop painful thoughts. A Bible verse came to my mind. "Let the peace of God that surpasses all understanding guard your heart and mind in Christ Jesus!" I thought about each word: God's ~ peace ~ surpasses ~ all ~ my understanding ~ guard ~ my heart ~ my mind ~ in Christ Jesus. . . . But then, my mind shouted back, "Ethan will never enjoy all that you prepared for him! He's never coming home again!"

Pat's hand touched my head. Did I wake her? With her hand on my head, a new thought came—Jesus' words from John's Gospel. "Let not your heart be troubled. Trust me. Look, I have prepared a place for Ethan. A place your precious son will never have to leave, a place more glorious than any room you could have prepared for him, an everlasting home where you will also join us."

Another new thought came—Ethan has met the I AM. How much better to meet a person than to just read about them? Now Ethan kisses God's face! The garrisons of peace had arrived, and I could feel them fighting for my heart.

> "And the peace of God, which transcends all understanding, will guard your hearts and your minds in Christ Jesus. Finally, brothers and sisters, whatever is true, whatever is noble, whatever is right, whatever is pure, whatever is lovely, whatever is admirable—if anything is excellent or praiseworthy—think about such things. . . . And the God of peace will be with you." (Philippians 4:7–9, NIV)

Your mind can torment you, or it can be a means of comfort, as you decide what you will dwell on. Prayer and memorization of Bible verses enabled me to control my thoughts.

To Do: Memorize a verse of Scripture that gives you peace.

To Read: DAY–Philippians 4; WEEK–Philippians 4, Psalm 7–12; MONTH–Psalms 65–94

6. Reject the lies.

When we returned from Chicago to an empty house, I berated myself for my lack of faith. *You should have ignored your dream about Ethan leaving you! You should have ignored the coroner waiting in the hall!* Wasn't Hezekiah told that he would die? Yet he prayed in faith and God gave him fifteen more years. If you had great faith, God would have raised Ethan from the dead!

On a flight out of Cincinnati, a man of Chinese descent in a white shirt and necktie sat by me. With a smile, he handed me a business card. "That Bible verse," he said, smiling even wider, "has changed my life."

Printed on his business card was Galatians 2:16. "We are justified not by the works of the law but by the faith of Christ." I flipped the card over and saw Chinese writing—his business details?

"On the back of my card," he explained, "is the Chinese Bible translation of Galatians 2:16. It says, 'Believing in Christ,' as though it's our faith and not 'the faith of Christ.'" He shook his head. "When I realized it is Christ's faith,"—his voice accentuated *Christ's*—"and not mine, it revolutionized my relationship with God."

"That's a great verse," I replied, working my smile muscles.

"It took the burden of believing off of me," he added. "It's not a matter of me mustering up my faith, but rather Christ's perfect faith at work in me."

How ironic being on the receiving end when talking about Christ. What were the chances of that guy sitting next to me? And how many times have I been that guy? God wanted me to know: "Mark, it's not a matter of you mustering up enough faith to raise your son from the dead. It wasn't my will to send Ethan back."

"Then you will know the truth, and the truth will set you free." (John 8:32, NIV)

There are many lies that will try to get between you and God, a lie such as that you could have somehow prevented a tragedy from happening or that God is punishing you. When you are hurting, the biggest lie you can believe is that God does not love you (Hebrews 5:7–11).

When the dirt comes down, as it did on that old donkey stuck in a well (the story I told in chapter 19), you need the truth of God's word. Then you can shake off the dirt and step up into a higher realm of living.

To Do: Replace half-truths with the absolutes of Scripture.

To Read: DAY–John 8; WEEK–John 8, Psalm 13–18;
 MONTH–John 8, Psalms 95–124

7. *Be willing to receive comfort.*

Johnathan drove Pat and me back to Cincinnati. Nathan and Elesha followed in Ethan's car. As I stretched out in the back seat, I never wanted to see Chicago again. My soul was traumatized. Once back in Ohio, we stopped to eat at Bella's Restaurant in Loveland, and Nathan's wife, Perry, met us with their new puppy. They had not named him yet, having brought him home the day Ethan died. Taking the puppy from Perry, I sensed that this little guy with big feet was scared. He looked at me with his deep blue eyes, and as I scratched a patch of white around his belly, I felt a strange sense of comfort.

> "All his sons and daughters came to comfort him, but he refused to be comforted. 'No,' he said, 'I will continue to mourn until I join my son in the grave.'" (Genesis 37:35, NIV)

To Do: Open your heart to receive comfort and love from God and others.

To Read: DAY–Genesis 24; WEEK–Genesis 24, Psalms 19–24;
 MONTH–Psalms 125–150, Revelation 4–5, 14, 21

8. Honor God.

The day after we returned from Chicago, we attended a vigil for Ethan where his friends gathered. A young man said, "My mother was struggling with her faith. She couldn't understand why God allowed pain and suffering. Well, I told Ethan about her struggle, and he sent me a paper he wrote on the subject. After I talked it through with my mom, she shed a few tears, and I could tell it made an impact on her. When I told Ethan, he was so happy, and he thanked me for letting him know. A few days later he texted me, saying, 'I'm praying for your mom.'"

At the vigil, I had the opportunity to share the gospel. I told Ethan's friends: "The reason I know Ethan is safely in heaven is not because of the good things he did or because he was such a nice guy. It is because of what Jesus did for him. Ethan would want each of us to know for certain that we will join him in heaven one day because Christ died for us."

When David saw that his servants were whispering, David perceived that the child was dead. Therefore David said to his servants, "Is the child dead?" And they said, "He is dead." So David arose from the ground, washed and anointed himself, and changed his clothes; and he went into the house of the LORD and worshiped. (2 Samuel 12:19–20)

To Do: Honor God in your pain. Make it count!

To Read: DAY–Revelation 21; WEEK–Revelation 21, Psalms 24–29;

MONTH–Luke 1–24, James 1–5, Philemon

9. Let others know.

Outside the post office near our home, I lifted mail bags into a cart on wheels, mailbags full of copies of *My African Dream*. Everyone on our mailing list would receive a copy, along with Ethan's memorial program. Then, I slipped a copy of the service inside a book for

Renitta, the postal worker who helps me post our monthly newsletter, and wheeled the cart through two sets of swinging doors. Renitta, as usual, was in the back. She looked surprised to see me with a big cart full of mail bags.

"I went downtown to the mail center," I called to her across the room. "Got instructions on how to send my books bulk rate."

"Okay, let's see what you got."

She punched buttons on her desktop PC for the required forms. Reaching into the cart, she opened a bag and pulled out several book packs, then back to the form she went.

"The ZIP codes are not in order," she said. "You'll have to sort them and bring them back."

"I'm not sure if I can do this right. We, um, buried our son yesterday," I blurted out.

She quickly looked up from her computer.

"He died," my voice went wobbly, "in a hammer throw accident."

She looked into my beleaguered eyes and said, "That was your son? I saw a picture of him on TV, but I didn't know that was your son!"

Awkwardly, I stooped to reach inside the cart. "I put his memorial service program inside the book I am mailing out. I wanted you to have a copy."

"Okay, I'm going to help you!" She placed her book on a table. "We'll get it right."

Her compassion for me stirred a torrent of feelings as I opened and closed my eyes rapidly and just managed to contain a floodgate of tears. Meanwhile, Renitta emptied a large bag of books onto the floor and, over the next hour, helped me get them in the right order. Later, when I finally got back to my car, I wept out loud.

"So they sat down with him on the ground seven days and seven nights, and no one spoke a word to him, for they saw that *his* grief was very great." (Job 2:13)

People need to know what you are going through. Just as dogs wag their tails or bark to let everyone know whether they are happy or upset, we need to let people know when we are grieving. Then they can relate to us with that understanding.

To Do: Let people whom you see regularly know that you are grieving.

To Read: DAY–Genesis 37; WEEK–Genesis 37, Isaiah 40–46; MONTH–Genesis 37, 49–50, Isaiah 40–66

10. *Find a place to cry.*

Every day for a month after Ethan died, I got in my car and cried—sometimes as soon as I started the engine, other times as I pulled out of the driveway. I restrained myself until I got out of the house because I did not want to sadden Pat at the start of her day by letting her see me cry.

Pat's grief was delayed, but by December, it was in full bloom. Pat, Elesha, and I were eating lunch together in our dining room one afternoon, and the approach of Christmas felt more like an appointment with a heart doctor than a celebration of the Advent of Christ.

"Ethan looked forward to Christmas. He was still like a child that way," Pat said. "A couple of years ago, Ryan Mecum told me, 'I don't know what you modeled for your sons in Africa, but it's like they're part of our Young Life leadership.' That was such a compliment. For me," Pat continued, "the hardest thing is not being his mother anymore, not seeing him fully developed."

Pat's face reddened and tears filled her eyes. Elesha set her fork down and cried. Closing my eyes, I felt them moisten like rain clouds filling. When I opened them, I felt the sting of tears. My tears came with such ease now—I never thought I would be able to cry like my girls. Tears communicate shared pain more than words ever could. Laughing is fun, but crying together bonds hearts as one, and tears anoint eyes to see the world in ways that dry eyes cannot.

That afternoon, Shirley Stoll, a friend for many years, emailed me: "Please tell Pat that I felt her mother's heart. Our children are developing like they did when they were in our wombs, and we allow God to complete what he began. Yes, Ethan will be fully developed, so you'll be astounded when you see him again."

It was as if Shirley had heard our lunchtime conversation!

"God, you have collected all my tears in your bottle." (Psalm 56:8, NLT)

Your tears are precious to God. No two teardrops are alike; they look different under a microscope and have different enzymes. Tears from a hard laugh look different from tears of sorrow—and tears are better released than suppressed; they drain pain like an anesthesia. So, cry often, knowing that Jesus wept, as did David, a warrior king who often spoke of his tears (more than 100 times, in fact). When you grieve deeply, you will find deep comfort because God responds to your tears. (Psalm 6:7; 13:3; 31:9–10; 38:6–9)

To Do: Find a place where you can cry and/or a person you can cry with.

To Read: DAY–Psalm 31; WEEK–Psalm 31, Psalms 13, 38, 42, 56, 80, 116;

MONTH–Psalm 31, Psalms 13, 38, 42, 56, 80, 116, 126,

Isaiah 25, 38, Jeremiah 9, 13, 14, Lamentations 1–5,

Ecclesiastes 1–12

---

11. *Take time to grieve.*

My attachment to Ethan—caring for him daily for nineteen years, enjoying his company, dreaming of all that he would become—caused me to feel his death in every fiber of my being. You do not stop loving a person when they die; your love intensifies.

"Grief," Patrick O'Malley quoted in *Getting Grief Right*, "really is love weeping, whether outward tears or a weeping heart."[8] Grief is healthy. It is not some bad emotion to avoid at all costs. Because it hurts, however, it is normal to suppress your grief; yet embracing it is wise (Ecclesiastes 7:2).

"Then Job got up and tore his clothes in grief. He shaved his head and threw himself face downward on the ground." (Job 1:20 GNT)

Sadness, anger, loneliness, and questions are not incompatible with faith in Christ. Jesus himself experienced these and more. Only one thing will you find in the Bible about wrong grief—do not grieve "without hope" (1 Thessalonians 4:13–18). You may even do strange things that you can't explain, like me not locking the door those first few nights. That's okay. Be patient with yourself.

To Do: Give yourself time to grieve your loss.

To Read: DAY–1 Thessalonians 4; WEEK–1 Thessalonians 4, Isaiah 47–52; MONTH–1 Thessalonians 4, Genesis 23, 27, 37, 50, Numbers 20, Deuteronomy 21, 26, 34, 1 Samuel 1–2, 15–16, 2 Samuel 1–2, 13–19, Proverbs 14, Hosea 4, 9, 10, Luke 8, 23, Revelation 1, 18

---

12. Recall the precious times.

The Christmas lights in Naperville, Illinois, were stunning, and we ended up at Lou Malnati's Pizzeria on Jefferson Avenue, eating bowls of salad while we waited for our deep-dish pizza. The place was hopping, and Ethan and I were in no hurry as we watched the Texans and the Raiders in an NFL playoff game. Bringing pizza to our table, the waiter apologized for our long wait and told us the pizza was "on the house." Ethan liked Chicago, its energy, its diversity. I liked the free pizza.

On our way back from his club's national championship soccer games in Oklahoma, Ethan and I stopped in St. Louis to watch the Reds play the Cardinals. We were seated in the left field bleachers at Busch Stadium when, in between innings, a St. Louis T-shirt was jettisoned into the stands—right at me. The Cardinals have a baseball dynasty, so when I caught the T-shirt, I said, "Maybe if I sleep in this, I'll wake up a St. Louis fan and enjoy baseball more." Ethan slowly shook his head from side to side. "Dad," he said, "it doesn't work that way!" As a Liverpool soccer fan, Ethan wouldn't dream of changing teams.

"Oh, that I were as in months past . . . When my children were around me; When my steps were bathed with cream, And the rock poured out rivers of oil for me!" (Job 29:1, 5–6)

Writing was a way for me to spend time with Ethan and relive some precious moments, because they ended too soon and abruptly. For you, it may mean doing something like what Pat did, putting a photo album together.

To Do: Let your mind take you back to that precious time.

To Read: DAY–2 Samuel 23; WEEK–2 Samuel 23, John 1–6;

        MONTH–2 Samuel 23, Proverbs 4, 8, John 1–21, Galatians 1–6

13. Journal your story of love.

Patrick O'Malley's book encouraged me to find my story of love in the sorrow of my loss. Others have also been comforted in their losses by creating something precious in the wake of grief. Ken Burns, the famous documentarian, said, "There was never a time growing up that I wasn't anxious about my mom dying." Ken's mother battled breast cancer from the time he was two years old until she died when he was eleven. Ken's father-in-law, a psychologist, told him, "Your whole life's work is an attempt to make people come back to life."[9] I understand that!

"Oh, that my words could be recorded. Oh, that they could be inscribed on a monument." (Job 19:23, NLT).

Life's greatest loves and losses must be recorded because you learn more from them than you do from your victories (Philippians 3:4–12). When Ethan died, I determined that I would not pastor again until I had recorded my son's life. Who else would record his life? For two years, I wrote for five hours a day while I itinerated on weekends and made mission trips overseas.

To Do: Start a journal; get something down on paper or record your experiences on audio. Find a way to express your feelings.

To Read: DAY–Job 19; WEEK–Job 19, Isaiah 8, 30, Jeremiah 30–32, Ezekiel 41–42, 2 Corinthians 3; MONTH–Proverbs 1–5, Isaiah 8, 30, Jeremiah 30–32, Joel 1–3, 2 Corinthians 3, Romans 1–16

14. Be thankful for something.

My first thankful thought: *Ethan was not left in a coma.* Also, I was thankful he went fast. Pat had a dream in which she saw a foot wearing a sock and a gym shoe quickly step onto a bus. "That's how fast Ethan left this world," God showed her. A student wrote, "I saw Ethan being welcomed into glory. He looked at God and God at him, and his face was radiant."

"In everything give thanks; for this is the will of God in Christ Jesus for you." (1 Thessalonians 5:18)

Giving thanks to God for the good in your life facilitates comfort. It is an antidote to resentment. Although it is hard to do this at first, you can find something to thank God for as you remember the good. You can thank God that he brings his children home, where they live without needs or wants. Heaven is the best long-term place to be for all of us.

To Do: Find something for which you can thank God.

To Read: DAY–1 Thessalonians 5; WEEK–1 Thessalonians 5, Leviticus 7, 2 Samuel 7, 1 Timothy 1–4; MONTH–1 Chronicles 16, Ezra 3, Nehemiah 11–12, Daniel 2, 1 Thessalonians 1–5, 1 Timothy 1–6, Acts 1–14

15. Expect divine appointments.

Two weeks after Ethan died, Pat and I joined a line of people under an oval-shaped yellow sign that read "Eggs and Things" in black letters.

When we reached the steps to the restaurant's entrance, a hostess handed us breakfast menus and asked, "Would you like to sit at the breakfast bar?"

"Yes," Pat answered, and I thought, *She's really hungry.* She never agrees to eat at the counter. Neither of us do, and I can't remember us ever eating at a restaurant counter.

On the right side of the restaurant, a dark laminated countertop ran the length of the wall. Of the eight seats, two were open. After we ordered, Pat started talking to the woman seated to her right. Soon she had the attention of the man on the other side of the woman as well. I did not hear what she said, but I hoped she wasn't telling them about Ethan. I did not want to talk to strangers about it. The couple, however, turned their heads toward me. "We're so sorry to hear about your son," the woman said, and the man nodded his head in sympathy.

I could not believe Pat had told them. But Pat looked at me with probing eyes and said in an explanatory tone, "When I heard them talk about worship, I just knew they were pastors. This is Murlene and Terry Sprenkel from Oregon."

Murlene, whose short brown hair was in a wispy shag, and Terry, who sported a gray buzz cut, were in their sixties. They had friendly faces and warm brown eyes. Pat and Murlene continued talking while I ate, occasionally glancing up and forcing a smile. When I finished my meal, I discovered that Pat had arranged for us to talk outside as couples.

"Four years ago, I died from a heart attack," Terry said as he gazed into the sky beyond us. "My spirit left my body. I felt peace like I'd never known. There was no shame or guilt. I was enveloped by pure beauty and love. God asked me, 'Do you want to stay or go back?' Everything in me wanted to stay, but out of my mouth came, 'Lord, your will be done.' The next thing I knew, I was descending and re-entering my body. It was like going into black sludge and heaviness."

Pat and I looked at one another but neither of us ventured a word.

"I'd put off every earthly thing that pollutes us and all that separates us from perfect union with God." Terry's eyes moistened. "Now I was back in this body of death. For weeks, I fought depression. Why had I come back? I longed for heaven like a person longs for happiness."

I stood amazed. God had arranged this meeting. Terry told us what it was like to die, have his spirit leave his body, want to stay in heaven, and then sadly return to the earth. Did Ethan's spirit look down on the Lawson Field? Did he see his injured body and those who frantically attended to him? Did he see the teams kneel and pray? When the paramedics got his pulse back, did God ask him if he wanted to stay? Can I not be happy for my son?

When you are in the wilderness of loss, tempted by the devil and not seeing things clearly, God will send ministering angels to you.

"Then, as they were afraid and bowed their faces to the earth, they said to them, 'Why do you seek the living among the dead?'" (Luke 24:5)

To Do: Expect divine appointments and look for God (co)incidences.

To Read: DAY–1 Samuel 9; WEEK–Exodus 3, 1 Samuel 9, Proverbs 19, Isaiah 46, Jeremiah 29, Acts 9, 17; MONTH–Exodus 3, 1 Samuel 9, Proverbs 19, Jeremiah 29, Philippians 1–4, Revelation 1–22

16. Get away.

Months before Ethan's accident, I had booked a vacation with Delta SkyMiles. "We must still go," I told Pat. "It'll help." Embracing my urge to escape, I viewed my previous booking as providential. It was because we met Terry and Murlene in Honolulu, Hawaii.

"We want to take you on a drive around the island," Terry said after we met at breakfast. He undid the latches and brought down the top on his convertible. The bright sun and cloudless sky reminded me of happier days in Zimbabwe. A gull screeched as we pulled onto a main road. At a stoplight, the smell of garlands wafted through the air and a forest of trees decorated the distant hillsides. Closer by, big-leaf tropical plants and palm trees trimmed the roadside with various shades of green, accompanied by patches of yellow and red vegetation. Terry turned into a parking lot where eager tourists walked to a viewing point. We strolled past a stand of mangos, papayas, and star fruit. Pat and Murlene ambled behind us, deep in conversation. The concrete viewing area provided an ocean vista of rich hues of brilliant blue. The colors stretched on forever.

We drove some more, and our ocean view was blocked by protruding hills, and then around a bend, the dazzling sea greeted us again, captivating me with a vibrant seascape of blue shades kissing a spotless sky at the horizon. Terry pulled into a turnaround on the edge of a cliff. The ocean danced beneath us in glittering beauty and rippling waves. The vivid royal blue mixed with aquamarine green and patches of dark blue. Large waves rushed to the waiting shoreline and crashed against the black lava rock, too distant to hear. Pockets of white mist sprayed upward.

To think that violent volcanic eruptions created these islands!

We descended from the lookout to the shoreline and jumped out of the white convertible. Like children off to play in the dreamlike crystal waters, Pat and Murlene took off their shoes. Terry and I followed their prudent and pretty lead. The warm sand squished under my toes, and my calf muscles tightened to keep me balanced and moving. Waves flowed over my feet. The water felt cool and refreshing. A few steps farther along, a warm current surprised me. Touched by beauty from every direction, I could almost forget that my heart was broken. What must Paradise be like? What are Ethan's eyes seeing right now? What is his heart experiencing?

On the way back, we sat and savored green, red, blue, and yellow flavored syrups. The sweet liquid was poured over snowlike ice with bits of soft, tart ice cream. The ice cream roused my taste buds with each mouthful. I had never had a "shave ice" before, but it tasted like a snow cone—except the ice was not crunchy, and the syrup was mixed better with the shaved ice.

Finding a healthy escape from grief, especially in the early days, can be helpful. Maybe a short vacation, for example. But remember, counterfeit escapes such as drugs, alcohol, and other unhealthy choices offer only temporary relief from pain. Let God provide you with a wholesome getaway to calm your mind.

"Come with me by yourselves to a quiet place and get some rest." (Mark 6:31, NIV)

After Jesus learned that his cousin, John, had been martyred, he and his disciples "withdrew by boat privately to a solitary place" (Matthew 14:12–13, NIV).

To Do: If you are able, get away for a while for a change of scenery.

To Read: DAY–Mark 6; WEEK–Mark 6–7, 2 Timothy 1–4, Philemon; MONTH–Acts 14–28, Mark 1–13, 2 John, 3 John, Jude

17. *Comfort those who hurt.*

The booths and tables were all taken at the Cheesecake Factory; the place was packed with hungry people waiting for seats and waiters hurrying about with trays. Pat and I were seated adjacent to an older woman who was by herself. Pat got her attention and said, "Hi, I'm Pat. My husband is Mark." Pat could talk to whomever she wanted to after introducing me to Terry and Murlene.

"I am Lindsay. I'm from New Zealand," she said with a Kiwi accent.

"Is this your first trip to Hawaii?" I asked.

"My husband and I were here two years ago. We planned another visit." She hesitated and then added, "But he died last year in an accident. Our car was swept away by a flash flood."

Was I hearing right?

"We're so sorry," Pat said. "You were together when it happened?"

"Oh, yes! Awful images kept appearing in my mind. For months I had trouble sleeping."

"Our son died," Pat said softly, "two and a half weeks ago, in an accident." She paused to complete her thought. "I think God put us next to you. He wants you to know he's with you."

Lindsay's eyes widened, and she told us of her grief as though she had never told a soul about her life's greatest loss, her love of fifty years gone. I felt great empathy for her.

" 'Comfort, yes, comfort My people!' says your God."
(Isaiah 40:1, TLB)

By measuring out comfort, you will also be comforted (2 Corinthians 1:1–7). Opportunities to comfort others will come, opportunities to pray for and reach out to others who are hurting.

To Do: Send a card, text, or email; make a phone call; or visit someone who is hurting.

To Read: DAY–Isaiah 40; WEEK–1 Kings 13–14, 21, Ecclesiastes 3, 7, 12, Daniel 10; MONTH–Haggai 1–2, Matthew 1–28

18. Spend time with loved ones.

On our return from Honolulu, Pat and I visited Johnathan and Holly in San Francisco. Elesha also flew out to meet us for Mother's Day. At Muir Woods, redwood trees welcomed us with cool shade, shooting upward like skyscrapers. Thin shafts of white light found their way through a canopy of foliage, falling serenely on green patches of ground cover. The tree bark was etched with grooves, and on the forest floor lay broken branches. A two-tiered wooden fence made from less majestic trees bordered our pathway, leading us along a creek of shallow pools and stones. We stopped by a large fallen tree that had been separated from its jagged trunk; to reach around its diameter, all five of us needed to stretch and join our hands.

More mounds and a stone bridge beckoned us over the winding creek, and the wooden path gave way to a dirt trail. We stopped at a huge stump, cut down by foresters and polished. The stump exposed the tree's rings and its incremental growth. Being the oldest living things on the planet, some sequoias were seedlings when Christ walked the earth. Only a third of the way through the stump, I recognized a date: Jamestown 1607. It was as if this dead giant spoke to me: *A life of twenty or ninety years—what's the difference compared to 2,000? And compared to eternity, every human life is a fleeting breath, a vapor that appears for a little while and is soon gone.*

Your loss can help you bond more closely with those you love because you have experienced the same loss. Pat and I have certainly bonded more deeply, and at times, it has seemed as if Ethan were whispering in my ears, "Love my mommy!" The love of family and friends has been my greatest source of earthly comfort. I pity those who are all alone in their loss (Ecclesiastes 4:9–12).

"There they made Him a supper; and Martha served, but Lazarus was one of those who sat at the table with Him." (John 12:2)

Precious times with loved ones help us live and face death. Before Jesus' crucifixion, he spent time with those he loved. In Bethany, he ate with Lazarus and his family, and in Jerusalem, he celebrated the Last Supper with his disciples.

To Do: Take additional time with your loved ones.

To Read: DAY–John 12; WEEK–John 7–13; MONTH–1 Corinthians 1–16, 2 Corinthians 1–13, Philemon

---

19. Beware of emotional ambushes.

I awoke on July 12, 2017—Ethan's birthday—three months after he died. He would have been twenty years old. No celebration now, and I felt great sadness. I just wanted to go back to sleep. Then I wondered, what's Ethan doing today? *He is having a party in heaven.* The answer was accompanied by familiar faces: my dad, Pat's dad, and others. On the windowsill in our dining room, the title of a book, *There's a Party in Heaven,*[10] jumped out at me, as if to confirm that soothing voice. Our friends Vince and Tricia Woltjer had sent us the book with a note: "Sometimes children's books describe it best."

When the first anniversary of Ethan's death approached, a book on grief warned me about possible emotional ambushes. I understood the concept, because earlier in February I had been ambushed while waiting for a connecting flight to Nepal. A young man reminded me of Ethan, and as if from nowhere, profound sorrow engulfed me. I had to find a nearby restroom.

"But the son of Paul's sister heard of their ambush, and he came and entered the barracks and told Paul." (Acts 23:16)

To Do: Plan something or do nothing on those special days.

To Read: DAY–Leviticus 23; WEEK–Leviticus 23, Judges 11, Matthew 26, Mark 14, Luke 2, John 2, 23; MONTH–Genesis 1–30

---

20. Write down what you believe God has shown you.

Nick Aldridge, a friend in Zimbabwe, sent me an email: "A song came to me for you: Kari Jobe's 'I Am Not Alone.'" The song speaks of God's light breaking through deep sorrow, and Nick didn't know that the father of Kari Jobe came up to Ethan after we had attended a service at Gateway Church in Dallas. He singled Ethan out among hundreds of people and inquired about his life.

God, the source of all comfort, promises to comfort you in your heartache (Matthew 5:4). Therefore, when you hurt, you need to connect deeply with him, because he wants to show you things that will comfort you (Matthew 7:7).

I have narrated the more pronounced ways God has spoken to my family. How he speaks to you will be equally unique and special. God speaks in many ways: through the Scriptures, a still soft voice, books, situations, even animals. But mostly, God speaks through people. The Bible is simply and profoundly the record of God speaking to people (Habakkuk 2:1–4). He spoke to every personality type in the Bible. God still speaks today. Make a note of what he says to you and refer to it often, because we tend to forget the details, especially when our heart is broken and time marches on.

> "Many have undertaken to draw up an account of the things that have been fulfilled among us." (Luke 1:1, NIV)

Even three years after Ethan's death, God continues to comfort us in new ways. Recently, my niece Rachel shared one of her dreams: "I dreamt that Colleen [Rachel's sister] and I were sitting at a table with my cousins Nathan and Johnathan. We were at a restaurant together for lunch. All of a sudden, my cousin Ethan, who passed away, appeared in an empty chair. He noticed that I was the only one who could see him. He smiled, waved, and said, 'Hi, Rachel!' I gasped and covered my mouth. Then he said, 'I am exactly where I'm supposed to be,' and disappeared. I immediately started crying."

Rachel did not know that I had recently written a book chapter entitled "An Empty Chair." And trust me—what Ethan said to her in her dream is vintage Ethan, even his smiling and waving.

To Do: Record what you believe God has said to you.

To Read: DAY–Luke 1; WEEK–Luke 1–2, Philippians 1–5; MONTH–Genesis 31–50, Exodus 1–10

---

21. *Recognize that everyone goes through sorrows.*

Tim and Rhonda, our friends of forty years, faced a diagnosis that their coming grandchild would not be "normal." Instead of being filled with joyful anticipation, the baby's birth was a time of anxiety and sad feelings of loss. Jen and Luke named their daughter Charlotte Joy, and the family fondly call her Charlie. She was born with Down syndrome. Jen, her mother, has since written a book titled *Chosen for Charlie*. No, at first they didn't feel chosen. They felt fearful as questions raced through their minds. But God spoke to Jen's heart: "I chose you for Charlie." In parenting Charlie, Jen and Luke have found that answer a source of grace. It has freed them from tormenting questions, so they can focus on doing everything they can to help Charlie fulfill her God-given purpose on earth.

God gives grace and grants his people redemptive answers. Those answers will always agree with the Bible. They will never claim that things just happen beyond God's power to control, because the Bible teaches that God is all-powerful (Psalm 115:3; 1 Chronicles 29:12; Proverbs 16:4, 33). He oversees the conception and formation of children in their mothers' wombs (Psalm 139:13; Jeremiah 1:5; Ecclesiastes 11:5; Job 31:15). "Chromosomal abnormalities" are subject to his purposes. He allows them for redemptive reasons and promises to bring good out of our pain (Exodus 4:11).

Jesus himself knew he was going to raise Lazarus from the dead, and yet, at Lazarus' tomb, Jesus wept with Mary and Martha. This is the shortest verse in the Bible, and yet it speaks volumes: "Jesus wept" (John 11:35).

To Do: Realize you are not alone in your suffering.

To Read: DAY–John 11; WEEK–1 Peter 1–5, 2 Peter 1–2;
     MONTH–1 Peter 1–5, Exodus 11–35

22. *Read other grief journey accounts.*

Reading accounts of those who have journeyed the terrain of grief will help you understand your grief and avoid hurtful expectations (Ecclesiastes 3:1–8). Here are a few:

Getting Grief Right: Finding Your Story of Love in the Sorrow of Loss
   by Patrick O'Malley and Tim Madigan

Why? Answers to Weather the Storms of Life by Vernon Brewer

Colors of Goodbye: A Memoir of Holding On, Letting Go, and
   Reclaiming Joy in the Wake of Loss by September Vaudrey

Grieving Dads: To the Brink and Back by Kelly Farley and David
   DiCola

Gone but Not Lost: Grieving the Death of a Child by David W.
   Wiersbe

"Clearly you are an epistle of Christ . . . written not with ink but by
the Spirit of the living God, not on tablets of stone but on tablets of
flesh, that is, of the heart." (2 Corinthians 3:3)

To Do: Order a book and/or read articles on grief and loss.

To Read: DAY–2 Corinthians 3:3; WEEK–2 Corinthians 3:3, Isaiah
   60–66; MONTH–2 Peter 1–3, 2 Thessalonians 1–3, Colossians
   1–4, 2 Timothy 1–4, Titus 1–3, Hebrews 1–13

---

23. *Realize people grieve differently.*

Pat would tell strangers about Ethan; not me, unless I had a good
reason to bring it up. Pat finds comfort going through Ethan's pictures,
while I find comfort in writing. Ethan's words, "I am from brown eyes
and black hair. I am from Mark and Pat," brought me to tears, yet it
made Pat smile. I smiled, however, when Pat recalled Ethan looking at
her wedding pictures and saying, "Mom, you were so pretty!" but she
barely got the words out before her tears flowed. It disturbed me when
I read that Ethan was laughing moments before the hammer struck
him, whereas Pat said, "I'm glad he was happy before he died." How
different is that?

"When the wife of Uriah heard that Uriah her husband was dead,
she mourned for her husband." (2 Samuel 11:26)

To Do: Remember that people are unique and handle loss differently.

To Read: DAY–2 Samuel 11; WEEK–2 Samuel 1–3, 11, 19, Haggai 1–2;
Month–2 Samuel 1–3, 11, 19, Zechariah 1–14, Amos 1–4, Joel
1–3, Malachi 1–4

24. *Seek resolutions.*

Students to our right lifted a banner: "Be Bold and Go All In." Cheers—
back and forth the ball went. Ten minutes into the game, a train roared
by on the hill opposite us and muzzled the hum of the crowd. Wheaton
and St. Olaf were scoreless at half time. We had spoken at chapel earlier
in the day, and that evening, we watched their opening soccer game.
In the second half, a Wheaton striker found the back of the net and
pointed to the patch on his arm. Two more goals followed. With each
goal, the Wheaton player pointed to his ER patch. When the whistle
blew to end the game, Jack, Ethan's teammate, leaped over a security
fence and climbed up into the stands to give Pat a hug. Johnathan
turned to me. "I'll never forget this," he said.

Ethan's death provoked not only the "Why, God?" question but also
questions of *how* it happened. Bouncing back and forth like the soccer
ball, we corresponded with the college. Nathan didn't want us to pursue
the matter with Wheaton. He had grace to walk away. I couldn't drop
it. I needed grace to walk it out. And just as we grieve differently, our
consciences differ at times, and Nathan and I agreed to differ on how
we dealt with the college.

I looked to God with regard to the college. Thankfully, I found a
special lawyer, David Schwaner, who kicked the ball for us. He has
represented us well, playing the game with skill, and Wheaton College
acted honorably. My aim now is to do what I can to ensure that this
never happens to another family. The NCAA must protect young men
and women from tragic injuries or deaths and not treat the Hammer
Throw event like an orphan sport.

"If your brother or sister sins against you, go and point out their fault." (Matthew 18:15, NIV)

To Do: Communicate clearly and seek to resolve the matter in a redemptive way.

To Read: DAY–Matthew 18; WEEK–Matthew 18, 1 Corinthians 1–7; MONTH–Joshua 1–24, Habakkuk 1–3, Zephaniah 1–3

25. *Expect good to come from your loss.*

"And we know that all things work together for good to those who love God, to those who are the called according to *His* purpose." (Romans 8:28)

Before Ethan was born, I had claimed Romans 8:28. I once had students in my homiletics class prepare sermons based on Bible verses that encapsulated the themes of their lives. I told them, "My verse is Romans 8:28. 'All things work together for good to those who love God.' My proposition," I continued, "is that the very things that seem dead set against you will become the very things that God uses for your good." Back then, I had my list of bad things that God had turned around for good, but nothing close to the death of a child. Johnathan's seven weeks in the neonatal intensive care unit topped my list.

In my dark pit of grief after Ethan's death, Romans 8:28 was my first glimmer of light. For me, "All things work together for good" is not a trite cliché glibly uttered. It is a life preserver. It carries a heart through the floodgates of turbulent waters. I call it "God's Assurance Policy." Whatever may happen in our lives, God assures us of his love and power to redeem it. I believe it is the greatest promise God has given us this side of heaven, and in my life, it remains the greatest verse of comfort.

The only condition for you to qualify for that promise is that you love God. Genuine love for God, however, is purified by the fiery trials you endure. These trials prove your love for God, your family, and others (James 1:12). No wonder this promise is made amidst a catalogue of extremely bad things like violence, hunger, nakedness, persecution, and death.

God's promise to use what is bad for good was fully demonstrated in Christ's death. For in that, God used the greatest of evils, the murder of the Prince of Life, for the greatest possible good, giving eternal life to all who would trust him. God also vindicated Jesus by raising him from the dead and seating him at his right hand, enthroned with all authority. When Jesus returns to earth, the dead will be raised, and on that day, God's promise will be fulfilled to the nth degree. Our resurrection will complete the working of all things together for good.

Meanwhile, God works together a great exchange: Jesus' righteousness for our sins, his faith for our doubts, his strength for our weaknesses, his hope for our despair, his thoughts and ways for our thoughts and ways, his garment of praise for our spirit of heaviness, his peace for our turmoil, his joy for our sorrow, his gentle yoke of learning his humility for our oppressive yoke of selfish ambition, his eternal life for our mortal life, his answers for our questions, and his great good out of the worst of our evils. Ultimately, may he increase in our lives and we decrease.

It helps to know that you'll grow through your loss. You will know God better and have more of him in your life. He's the ultimate Father, who, in sharing with us procreation and parenting, shares his own heart. Through marriage and children, he teaches us love, and through suffering, he deepens that love. We might rather have a trouble-free life, but love and faith wouldn't grow strong that way.

My worst news is being transformed by God's best news, my worst pain exchanged for pleasures at his right hand, and my biggest loss traded for the best possible gain. The Father of Jesus Christ is so infinitely wise and good that he permitted Ethan's death to hurt me and my family only for a limited time in order to bring about a lasting good, which would never have existed otherwise, but will now continue without end. God called light out of darkness when he created the universe, and he has turned my darkness into light, a light that will shine brighter and brighter until the perfect day when I see a "thousand-thousand Ethans" in glory.

To Do: Look for the silver linings.

To Read: DAY–Romans 8; WEEK–Romans 8 for 7 days;

MONTH–Romans 8 for 30 days

---

26. Pursue God's purpose.

From the first day of your loss to the day God fully redeems it, God has a purpose.

"Look at this video," Elesha said, handing me her phone as she went to the breakfast bar. The video caption said, "An emotional goodbye: Teen sobs over loss of friend. Matthew remembers the last time he saw Ethan Roser."

Blond hair and bright eyes, Matthew could be a poster child for the All-American Boy. He is a Young Life leader who works with high school kids and tells them about Jesus. As the video began, the voice-over reports, "A Mason High School senior met up with Roser a month ago at Westshore Pizza. He never thought that meeting would be their last. Matthew says, 'I can't believe this happened, because he was such a good guy.'" Then Matthew breaks into sobs and a picture of Ethan appears. I grope for my teacup. Matthew appears again on the screen. "Ethan Roser was one of our heroes. We loved how much Ethan cared for his Mason friends to learn more about the life of Jesus Christ."

> "For I determined not to know anything among you except Jesus
> Christ and Him crucified." (1 Corinthians 2:2)

I find comfort in knowing that you will be comforted. May God minimize your troubles and maximize your comfort. When you face darkness, may he grant you vivid light so you can cooperate with his eternal purposes in Christ.

To Do: Discover what new things God has for you.

To Read: DAY–1 Corinthians 2; WEEK–1 Corinthians 2, 9, 1 John 1–5; MONTH–Deuteronomy 1–13, Numbers 1–17

27. *Think about heaven.*

Sitting on the sofa on what would have been Ethan's twentieth birthday, I perused Randy Alcorn's book *Heaven*,[11] the book where I had found the marker with Ethan's picture. On page 457, the heading read "Going to the Party."

> Imagine someone takes you to a party. You see a few friends there, enjoy a couple of good conversations, a little laughter, and some decent appetizers. The party's all right, but you keep hoping it will get better. . . . Suddenly, your friend says, "I need to take you home." *Now?* You're disappointed . . . but you leave, and your friend drops you off at your house. As you approach the door, you're feeling all alone and sorry for yourself. As you open the door and reach for the light switch, you sense someone's there. . . . "Surprise!" Your house is full of smiling people, familiar faces. It's a party—for you. . . . You recognize the guests, people you haven't seen for a long time. Then, one by one, the people you most enjoyed at the other party show up at your house, grinning. This turns out to be the *real* party.
>
> Christians faced with terminal illness or imminent death often feel they're leaving the party before it's over. They have to go home early. They're disappointed, thinking of all they'll miss when they leave. But the truth is, the real party is underway at home—precisely where they're going. They're

not the ones missing the party; those of us left behind are. . . . One by one . . . we'll disappear from this world. Those we leave behind will grieve that their loved ones have left home. In reality, however, their believing loved ones aren't *leaving* home, they're *going* home. They'll be home before us. We'll be arriving at the party a little later.

Alcorn's book assures me there's far more to heaven than I had imagined. Why don't we think and talk more about heaven? Is it because we have such a distorted picture of it? Many imagine heaven as a purposeless, disembodied existence, floating around in an abstract, ethereal realm. Who would want to go to such a place? But that image is as far from the truth as we can get. According to the Bible, there is a coming resurrection of our bodies and an unending life on a New Earth that God will create.

"Set your mind on things above." (Colossians 3:2)

To Do: Meditate on the joy and perfections that await you in heaven.

To Read: DAY–Colossians 3; WEEK–Colossians 3, 2 Corinthians 10, Revelation 4–5, 14, 21, Isaiah 6; MONTH–Ezekiel 1–30

28. Seek God's glory.

"Jesus said this to indicate the kind of death by which Peter would glorify God. Then he said to him, 'Follow me!'" (John 21:19, NIV)

We've heard many testimonies of how God has touched people through Ethan's death. What follows is a brief sampling of how Ethan's death has glorified God.

Will:

One year ago, I got a phone call: "Ethan Roser is no longer with us." That one sentence was enough to shatter me. There were many months full of pain and sorrow and confusion. . . . But your story, Ethan, isn't one of sorrow and confusion. Your story is hope and joy. You lived your life every single day for the Lord, and you helped me and many others want to do the same. You have proved to me that God can bring life through death. Ethan, you have inspired me to go public with my faith and show everyone that I meet that there is hope and joy in Jesus. You'll always be one of the most important parts of my story.

Dylan:

My mom and I got baptized this past weekend! I could have never done it without Ethan being in my life and influencing me to go through with it. I hope I can help push more and more of my friends to commit just like I have. Being able to talk with Mark and Pat this summer also opened up my eyes and helped me realize what I was missing.

Josh:

I was one of the captains of the Wheaton College soccer team and a friend to Ethan. His fever for Christ has inspired a significant change in my personal disposition toward Christ, but last night it came out in a very special way. I coach a public high school girls' soccer team in Birmingham. Last night at practice, I shared about my experience playing at Wheaton and about my friend Ethan, who loved people more than himself, who was a spark to anyone who met him, and most importantly, who loved the Lord. I hoped to plant a seed in at least one heart. The impact, however, has absolutely blown me away. For several girls, something about Ethan's story clicked in their heads. I've already had conversations ranging from "tell me more about all this" to sharing Christ. Seeds have been planted in many young hearts. Even though this team is undefeated and very serious about soccer, they decided to cancel practice in order to talk about Ethan's story and the gospel. They even created "Ethan's Rule," where teammates are required to only edify each other with their words.

To Do: Involve God in what you think, say, and do.

To Read: DAY-John 21; WEEK-John 21, Daniel 1–6;
  MONTH-Ezekiel 31–48, Song of Solomon 1–8, Ruth 1–4

29. *Anticipate new joy.*

When Ethan died, I wondered whether I would ever know joy again on this side of heaven. Grief touches on a whole mountain range of feelings, and I had to draw a line between my grief and self-pity. Grief can morph into feeling sorry for yourself. When it does, don't stay there. God can restore your joy. He has for me. A short school paper Ethan wrote at age ten hangs in my office, reminding me to laugh often.

The Day My Dad Laughed!

It all started when the phone rang. I answered, "Hello." "Is Johnathan there?" "No." Then Dad came on and said, "Hello, who is it?" "Mike Black." "Who?" "Mike Black." "Who?" "Mike Black." "Ethan, can you hear him?" "Yes, it's Mike Black asking if Johnathan Roser is here." Ahahaha! "John's in Tennessee." I hung up, and the next thing I know, Dad is laughing like a hyena. Hahahahahahahahahahahahahahaha! His face is red.

The harder I laughed, the funnier Ethan thought this was. We laughed nonstop for five minutes . . . and I laugh now because we will laugh together again someday soon!

"Therefore the redeemed of the LORD shall return, and come with singing unto Zion; and everlasting joy shall be upon their head: they

shall obtain gladness and joy; and sorrow and mourning shall flee away." (Isaiah 51:11, KJV)

To Do: Know that it's okay to laugh and enjoy what God gives you.

To Read: DAY–Isaiah 51; WEEK–Esther 8–9, Acts 2, 8, 13, 15, 20; MONTH–Esther 1–9, Deuteronomy 14–34, Isaiah 51

---

30. Keep going and growing.

In writing this book, I have grown. For one, Pat tells me, "You're more open and honest about how you feel." My writing was guided by that simple principle—God appears to us with real comfort when we are transparent with him and others.

I've wrestled with God many times. Often, I have contended with him about my situation. He knows, however, that we dwell in houses of clay. In the Bible, he does not gloss over faults in the lives of his people, whether it be Abraham and Sarah, Joseph and his brothers, David, or Peter and Paul.

In thinking about divulging faults, I have often considered Ethan's faults. I even asked Pat as well as Ethan's siblings and friends about what character flaws they had seen in him: Times of getting angry, stretching the rules, playing pranks, and being overboard about soccer were the worst of what we saw in him. Ethan was human and imperfect, but he was an unusually trouble-free person and lived an amazing life.

Initially, I debated about whether I should limit the story to *why* God allowed the accident and avoid the question of human culpability in *how* it happened. But again, God tells it like it is, and he relates the whole story so that in every circumstance of life we might trust him to turn our bad into good. Therefore, integrity demanded that I include the conflict with Wheaton College and the NCAA. Nothing I have written, however, is fabricated. Ethan is far too precious to me to make anything up, and my aim in telling the whole story is that you might find comfort in your losses.

> "Although I wrote to you, *I did* not *do it* for the sake of him who had done the wrong, nor for the sake of him who suffered wrong, but that . . . God might appear to you. Therefore, we have been comforted in your comfort." (2 Corinthians 7:12–13)

God is the source of all comfort, and there are many other means of comfort in addition to those listed here. You could get a puppy, find a diversion in a hobby, or throw yourself into a project, for example. I have shared these thirty points with the desire to help you in some small way. It is God who brought me the greatest comfort my soul has ever known, and I pray that as deep as your sorrow is, God's comfort in your life will be deeper still, so that you, too, may comfort others.

To Do: Live your life fully, because people need you.

To Read: DAY–Proverbs 1; WEEK–Proverbs 1, 3, 9, 11, 14, 16, 24; MONTH–Numbers 18–36, Ezra 1–10, Obadiah 1

THE FINAL WORD

All of creation is telling a story, and as in all good stories, there is plenty of drama. Now, as creation moves ever closer to the full light of eternity that awaits us all, may we rely on God more and more in our own stories, and may we get to know him better and better, just as Ethan described when he applied to serve at camp:

> When soccer was taken away from me, it gave me a chance to focus on what should have been at the center of my life all that time: my relationship to God and what he intended to make of my life. Without soccer, I had more time to give to my relationship with Christ other than simply going to church and youth group. He really took a hold of my life in a way I had never experienced before. My whole life I thought I had a close relationship with God, but it was during this time I learned to rely on him more. And the more I relied on him, the more I knew him and what his calling on my life meant.

I would love to hear your story and how God is comforting you.

To view pictures of Ethan, additional stories, videos, and more, visit Facebook: Ethan Roser Home Going Service.

To hear more about Ethan's and the Rosers' life in Africa, order *My Africa Dream* at mcroser.com.

To learn more about Mark's other books—*God's Sovereignty*, a study of God's rule over all of his creation; *The Cleansing of the Heavens*, a study of Satan's modus operandi and how Jesus' death defeated him; and *The Unsealed Book*, a study of the Book of Revelation—please visit mcroser.com.

NOTES

1 Eloise Wilkin and Jane Werner Watson, *My Little Golden Book About God* (New York: Random House Children's Books, 1993), 9-11.

2 Patrick O'Malley and Tim Madigan, *Getting Grief Right: Finding Your Story of Love in the Sorrow of Loss* (Boulder, CO: Sounds True, 2017).

3 Randy Alcorn, *Heaven* (Carol Stream, IL: Tyndale House, 2004.

4 This is my paraphrase to summarize this psalm.

5 Rebecca Springer, *Within Heaven's Gates* (New Kensington, PA: Whitaker House, 1984), 55.

6 https://www.christianitytoday.com/edstetzer/2017/may/in-memory.htm

7 Revelation 5:1–9, NIV.

8 Tim Lawrence, timlawrence.com//blog/2016/2/8/inadequate, quoted in O'Malley and Madigan, *Getting Grief Right*, 100.

9 Quoted in the *Los Angeles Times*, June 13, 2013: https://www.latimes.com/science/la-xpm-2013-jun-04-la-sci-sn-ken-burns-cancer-documentary-20130604-story.htm

10 Gary and Jan Bower, *There's A Party in Heaven* (Traverse City, MI: Bower Family Books, 2007).

11 Alcorn, *Heaven*, 457.

PERMISSIONS

Permission granted by Josh Gracin to use the lyrics to the song *I Can't Say Goodbye* from the recording *Redemption*.

Permission granted by Randy Alcorn to quote from his book *Heaven*.

Permission granted by Vineyard Music South Africa, Costa Mitchell and Pamela Shaw to use lyrics of song *Only You* by Andy Shaw.

ABOUT PARACLETE PRESS

WHO WE ARE

As the publishing arm of the Community of Jesus, Paraclete Press presents a full expression of Christian belief and practice—from Catholic to Evangelical, from Protestant to Orthodox, reflecting the ecumenical charism of the Community and its dedication to sacred music, the fine arts, and the written word. We publish books, recordings, sheet music, and video/DVDs that nourish the vibrant life of the church and its people.

WHAT WE ARE DOING

BOOKS | PARACLETE PRESS BOOKS show the richness and depth of what it means to be Christian. While Benedictine spirituality is at the heart of who we are and all that we do, our books reflect the Christian experience across many cultures, time periods, and houses of worship.

We have many series, including *Paraclete Essentials*; *Paraclete Fiction*; *Paraclete Poetry*; *Paraclete Giants*; and for children and adults, *All God's Creatures*, books about animals and faith; and *San Damiano Books*, focusing on Franciscan spirituality. Others include *Voices from the Monastery* (men and women monastics writing about living a spiritual life today), *Active Prayer*, and new for young readers: *The Pope's Cat*. We also specialize in gift books for children on the occasions of Baptism and First Communion, as well as other important times in a child's life, and books that bring creativity and liveliness to any adult spiritual life.

The MOUNT TABOR BOOKS series focuses on the arts and literature as well as liturgical worship and spirituality; it was created in conjunction with the Mount Tabor Ecumenical Centre for Art and Spirituality in Barga, Italy.

MUSIC | PARACLETE PRESS DISTRIBUTES RECORDINGS of the internationally acclaimed choir *Gloriæ Dei Cantores*, the *Gloriæ Dei Cantores Schola*, and the other instrumental artists of the *Arts Empowering Life Foundation*.

PARACLETE PRESS IS THE EXCLUSIVE NORTH AMERICAN DISTRIBUTOR for the Gregorian chant recordings from St. Peter's Abbey in Solesmes, France. Paraclete also carries all of the Solesmes chant publications for Mass and the Divine Office, as well as their academic research publications.

In addition, PARACLETE PRESS SHEET MUSIC publishes the work of today's finest composers of sacred choral music, annually reviewing over 1,000 works and releasing between 40 and 60 works for both choir and organ.

VIDEO | Our video/DVDs offer spiritual help, healing, and biblical guidance for a broad range of life issues including grief and loss, marriage, forgiveness, facing death, understanding suicide, bullying, addictions, Alzheimer's, and Christian formation.

Learn more about us at our website:
www.paracletepress.com
or phone us toll-free at 1.800.451.5006

SCAN
TO
READ

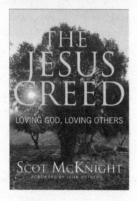